Contemporary Irish Writers

Contemporary Irish Writers and Filmmakers

General Series Editor:
Eugene O'Brien, Head of English Department,
Mary Immaculate College, University of Limerick.

Titles in the series:
Seamus Heaney: Creating Irelands of the Mind
by Eugene O'Brien (Mary Immaculate College, Limerick)

Brian Friel: Decoding the Language of the Tribe
by Tony Corbett

Jim Sheridan: Framing the Nation by Ruth Barton
(University College Dublin)

John Banville: Exploring Fictions by Derek Hand
(St. Patrick's College, Drumcondra, Dublin)

Neil Jordan: Exploring Boundaries by Emer Rockett and
Kevin Rockett (Trinity College Dublin)

Roddy Doyle: Raining on the Parade by Dermot McCarthy
(Huron University College, University of Western Ontario)

Conor McPherson: Imagining Mischief by Gerald Wood
(Carson-Newman College, Tennessee)

William Trevor: Re-imagining Ireland by Mary Fitzgerald-Hoyt
(Siena College, New York)

John McGahern: From the Local to the Universal by Eamon Maher
(Institute of Technology, Tallaght)

Forthcoming:
Jennifer Johnston by Shawn O'Hare

Brendan Kennelly by John McDonagh

Contemporary Irish Writers

William Trevor

Re-imagining Ireland

Mary Fitzgerald-Hoyt

The Liffey Press

Published by The Liffey Press
Ashbrook House, 10 Main Street,
Raheny, Dublin 5, Ireland
www.theliffeypress.com

© 2003 Mary Fitzgerald-Hoyt

A catalogue record of this book is
available from the British Library.

ISBN 1-904148-06-9

*This book has been published with the assistance of grant-aid
from An Chomhairle Ealaíon, The Arts Council of Ireland*

Printed in the Republic of Ireland by Colour Books Ltd.

Contents

About the Author

Mary Fitzgerald-Hoyt is Professor of English at Siena College in Loudonville, New York, where she teaches a variety of Irish literature courses. Her writings on Irish literature have appeared in *The Canadian Journal of Irish Studies*, *Etudes Irlandaises*, *New Hibernia Review*, *Colby Quarterly*, *Nua*, and *Notes on Modern Irish Literature*, among others. She is also a regular book reviewer for *The Irish Literary Supplement.*

For Don

Series Introduction

Given the amount of study that the topic of Irish writing, and increasingly Irish film, has generated, perhaps the first task of a series entitled *Contemporary Irish Writers and Filmmakers* is to justify its existence in a time of diminishing rainforests. As Declan Kiberd's *Irish Classics* has shown, Ireland has produced a great variety of writers who have influenced indigenous, and indeed, world culture, and there are innumerable books devoted to the study of the works of Yeats, Joyce and Beckett. These writers spoke out of a particular Irish culture, and also transcended that culture to speak to the Anglophone world, and beyond.

However, Ireland is now a very different place from that which figures in the works of Yeats, Joyce and Beckett, and it seems timely that the representations of this more secular, more European, and more cosmopolitan Ireland should be investigated and it is with this in mind that *Contemporary Irish Writers and Filmmakers* has been launched.

This series will examine the work of writers and filmmakers who have engaged with the contemporary cultural issues that are important in Ireland today. Irish literature and film has often been viewed as obsessed with the past, but contemporary writers and filmmakers seem to be involved in a process of negotiation between the Ireland of the past and the Ireland of the coming times. It is on this process of negotiation that much of our current imaginative literature and film is focused, and this series hopes to investigate this process through the chosen *auteurs*.

Indeed, it is a sign of the maturity of these *auteurs* that many of them base their narratives not only in the setting of this "new Ireland", but often beyond these shores. Writers and filmmakers such as Seamus Heaney, John Banville, William Trevor and Neil Jordan have the confidence to write and work as *artists* without the necessary addendum of the qualifying "Irish". Their concerns, themes and settings take them outside Ireland to a global stage. Yet, as this series attests, their "Irishness", however that is defined, remains intact and is often imprinted even in their most "international" works.

Politically and culturally, contemporary Ireland is in something of a values deficit as the previous hegemonic certainties of party political and religious allegiance have been lost in a plethora of scandals involving church and state. The role of art and culture in redefining the value-ethic for our culture has never been more important, and these studies will focus on the notions of Irishness and identity that prevail in the late twentieth and early twenty-first centuries.

The role of the aesthetic in the shaping of attitudes and opinions cannot be understated and these books will attempt to understand the transformative potential of the work of the artist in the context of the ongoing redefinition of society and culture. The current proliferation of writers and filmmakers of the highest quality can be taken as an index of the growing confidence of this society, and of the desire to enunciate that confidence. However, as Luke Gibbons has put it: "a people has not found its voice until it has expressed itself, not only in a body of creative works, but also in a body of critical works", and *Contemporary Irish Writers and Filmmakers* is part of such an attempt to find that voice.

Aimed at the student and general reader alike, it is hoped that the series will play its part in enabling our continuing participation in the great humanistic project of understanding ourselves and others.

Eugene O'Brien
Department of English
Mary Immaculate College
University of Limerick

Acknowledgements

This book could not have been completed without support from my friends, students, and colleagues at Siena College. Fr Kevin Mackin, President, and Linda Richardson, Chitra Rajan and Timoth Lederman, present and former Vice Presidents for Academic Affairs, granted me much-needed reassigned time from teaching. The Committee on Teaching and the Women's and Multicultural Studies Committee were generous with summer stipends. Ellen Johnson and Sue Kuebler always knew how to make the most uncooperative computer disks behave. Joe Patti and Lynne Daly offered invaluable technical support. I am grateful to my Irish Studies colleagues in the American Conference for Irish Studies (ACIS) and the International Association for the Study of Irish Literatures (IASIL) for allowing me to present my research at conferences as well as providing stimulating conversations and invaluable comradeship, and especially to Alex Gonzalez for years of friendship and encouragement.

Portions of this book have appeared in *Notes on Modern Irish Literature* and *Colby Quarterly*. I thank Edward Kopper, Editor of *NMIL*, and Douglas Archibald, Editor of *Colby Quarterly*, not only for their permissions but also for their close and sympathetic reading of my work.

For my family, especially my late parents, John W. Fitzgerald and Fredericka Tansey Fitzgerald, who instilled in me a love for my Irish heritage, and for the grandparents I never met, whose courage and struggle as immigrants continues to awe me, I am deeply indebted. Bernie Fitzgerald, my brother, has been infinitely patient with technological assistance.

I consider myself a lucky woman in my friendships. David Sonstroem deserves special mention for being my toughest and kindest writing mentor. Ed Howe's many years of encouragement are deeply appreciated. Seamus Blake has been unstintingly generous with his vast knowledge of Irish language and literature. Thanks to Christiane Farnan for steadfast support and for continuing to be her own dear self, and to Meg Woolbright for her many kindnesses.

Special thanks are due to Pam Clements for her loyal friendship, her honest criticism, and her much-needed sense of the ridiculous.

Finally, to Donald Carter Hoyt: an Irish expression is most appropriate: *cuisle mo chroí.*

Mary Fitzgerald-Hoyt
Siena College
New York
September 2003

Chronology

1928	William Trevor Cox is born on 24 May in Mitchelstown, County Cork, second of three children of James William Cox and Gertrude Davison Cox.
1941–46	Attends Sandford Park School, Dublin and St Columba's College, Dublin.
1946–50	Attends Trinity College, Dublin (BA in History).
1951–53	Teaches history in Armagh, Northern Ireland.
1952	Marries Jane Ryan.
1953–58	Moves to England; works as church sculptor; shares first prize in the Irish section of the "Unknown Political Prisoner" international sculpture competition; teaches art in Rugby; sons Patrick and Dominic born; one-man sculpture shows in Dublin and Bath.
1958	*A Standard of Behaviour* published.
1960–64	Works as advertising copywriter at Notley's, London.
1965	*The Old Boys* (1964) wins Hawthornden Prize; *The Boarding-House* published.
1966	*The Love Department* published.

1967	*The Day We Got Drunk on Cake and Other Stories* published.
1969	*Mrs Eckdorf in O'Neill's Hotel* is published and short-listed for the Booker Prize.
1971	*Miss Gomez and the Brethren* published.
1972	*The Ballroom of Romance and Other Stories* published; Trevor awarded Society of Authors travelling fellowship.
1973	*Elizabeth Alone* published.
1975	*Angels at the Ritz and Other Stories* published.
1976	*The Children of Dynmouth* wins the Whitbread Novel Award; Trevor wins the Allied Irish Banks Prize for fiction and the Heinemann Award for Fiction, and is short-listed for the Booker Prize; *Old School Ties* published.
1977	Made Honorary Commander of the British Empire.
1978	*Lovers of Their Time and Other Stories* published.
1979	*The Distant Past and Other Stories* published.
1980	*Other People's Worlds* published.
1981	*Beyond the Pale and Other Stories*; *Scenes From an Album* staged at the Abbey Theatre, Dublin.
1983	*Fools of Fortune* wins the Whitbread Novel Award; *The Stories of William Trevor* published.
1984	*A Writer's Ireland: Landscape in Literature* published; awarded honorary D. Litt., University of Exeter.
1986	*The News From Ireland and Other Stories* published.
1987	*Nights at the Alexandra* published.
1988	*The Silence in the Garden* wins a *Sunday Independent* Arts Award and is named *Yorkshire Post* Book of the Year.

1989	Edits *The Oxford Book of Irish Short Stories*.
1990	*Family Sins and Other Stories* published; Trevor awarded honorary D.Litt., National University, Cork.
1991	*Two Lives: Reading Turgenev and My House in Umbria* published; *Reading Turgenev* shortlisted for the Booker Prize; *Juliet's Story* published.
1992	*The Collected Stories* published; Trevor wins the *Sunday Times* Award for Literary Excellence.
1993	*Excursions in the Real World* published.
1994	*Felicia's Journey* wins Whitbread Book of the Year and *Sunday Times* Book of the Year; Trevor named a Companion of Literature by the Royal Society of Literature.
1996	*After Rain* published.
1997	Named to Aosdána.
1998	*Death in Summer* published.
1999	Wins Arts Council of England's David Cohen British Literature Prize for lifetime achievement.
2001	*The Hill Bachelors* wins *Irish Times* Literary Prize and the PEN/Macmillan Silver Pen Award for Short Stories.
2002	*The Story of Lucy Gault* shortlisted for the Man Booker Prize for Fiction and the Whitbread Novel Award.

List of Abbreviations

Introduction

It has become commonplace to describe William Trevor as one of the best short story writers of the twentieth century, if not *the* best; he is also a critically acclaimed novelist. A much-honoured author, having won such awards as the Whitbread Prize, the Hawthornden Prize, and *The Irish Times* Literary Prize, Trevor nevertheless remains under-considered by literary critics. Despite the fact that he has been writing for over forty years, only four previous book-length studies of his work have been published, and all of them have undertaken the daunting task of providing an overview of a prolific career.

Trevor's very versatility has perhaps contributed to the relatively modest output of critical studies: though Irish by birth, as a young man he emigrated to England, a setting that continues to figure largely in his work. Though Trevor has never returned to Ireland to live, feeling that the same distance that enabled him to first write about his homeland may have become a necessity in that writing's continuation, Ireland remains the inspiration for his best writing, and he considers himself to be an Irish writer. But here Trevor eludes easy categorisation: he writes with ease about Catholics, middle-class Protestants, the Big House culture, and the divided populace of Northern Ireland. Perhaps the very difficulty of placing Trevor has caused critics to neglect him.

Indeed, in a recent special issue of *Colby Quarterly* devoted exclusively to Trevor's work, editor Douglas Archibald expresses puzzlement that a writer who has written so incisively about Ireland for so many years has been virtually ignored by Irish literary critics.

Trevor's personal history ensured that he would come to view Ireland as a diverse, not a monolithic, country. Born William Trevor Cox in Mitchelstown, County Cork, in 1928, the author spent an itinerant childhood, mostly in southern and southwestern Ireland, relocations necessitated by his father's job as a bank official. Protestant by birth, he at one time attended an all-girls' Catholic school. Despite the fact that he came to see himself as belonging to a "withering" population of middle-class Protestants displaced by de Valera's Ireland, his understanding of Catholic Ireland is evident in his writing, as is, conversely, his shrewd insight into the contradictions and ironies of Big House culture, which in his childhood was well on its way to extinction. His mother was born in County Armagh, Northern Ireland, and Trevor once taught in a boys' school there. On the occasions when he has written about the North, he comprehends the depth and intricacy of the cultural fissures that define that troubled place.

When Trevor entered university at Trinity College, he chose History as his major field, and his familiarity with Irish history permeates his works. He began his artistic life as a sculptor, not a writer, and even here Ireland was a formative influence: his early carving was inspired by designs from the Book of Kells (MacKenna, 1999: 51).

Despite the fact that Trevor's Irish fiction is often connected thematically and stylistically to works set outside Ireland, it also stands alone as a sustained, evolving study on its own terms. As a young writer living an expatriate life in England, Trevor wrote primarily about the English, whom he found odd and alien, and his sense of being an outsider lent his writing about England a satiric edge and a love for the eccentric that bespeaks the influence of Charles Dickens, one of Trevor's favourite authors. But as time widened the distance between himself and his homeland, and as sectarian violence erupted on both islands, Trevor's emotional engagement with Ireland took hold, and since the late 1960s Ireland has remained a major preoccupation in his writing. Significantly, when Penguin repackaged selections from the *Collected Stories* into new paperback editions in the 1990s, the volumes were entitled *Ireland* and *Outside Ireland*.

Trevor's Irish writing includes short stories and novels, plays, screenplays, a memoir, and a non-fiction exploration of the impact of Irish places upon Irish writers. This study will focus almost exclusively on the fiction, not only because of space constraints but because it is the largest, most sustained body of Trevor's Irish writing.

Chapter One discusses Trevor's Dublin works, beginning with his first Irish novel, *Mrs Eckdorf in O'Neill's Hotel*, published in 1969. The novel was strongly influenced by James Joyce's *Ulysses*, tracing the activities of a series of peripatetic characters linked by a decaying hotel and its deaf-mute proprietor. A blend of broad comedy and poignancy, the novel reveals Trevor's early struggle to find a distinctively Irish voice. Yet here and in later short stories with Dublin settings, it is apparent that the author is working in a milieu in which he has never been completely comfortable. Although Trevor attended boarding school and university in Dublin, he has never been at home in the city, and in his later forays into Dublin fiction he seems more at ease depicting characters from provincial Ireland who, like himself, are outsiders. Further, the shadow of Joyce's *Dubliners*, a work Trevor admires, hangs heavily over the Dublin short stories, making it apparent that the author needed to find a way to impose his own vision of Ireland upon his fiction.

Chapter Two explores what Dolores MacKenna has described as "Trevor's Ireland", the small town and rural country of the author's youth. This is an Ireland of lonely souls with unfulfilled dreams, imaginative children in unsympathetic homes, lives constrained by poverty and limited opportunity. Trevor finds his own voice and setting in provincial Ireland. It is a setting he seldom abandons in his Irish fiction: even his explorations of Irish history and politics most often take place in provincial settings.

Though Trevor's earliest Irish short stories were inspired by the provincial Ireland he loves, in the late 1960s and the 1970s, as sectarian violence rocked Northern Ireland, Ireland's Troubles past and present increasingly preoccupied Trevor's fiction. Chapter Three deals with Trevor's early stories about the Troubles, stories wherein violence is contagious and history seems inexorably to repeat itself.

Although Protestant by birth, Trevor's family was unconnected to the Anglo-Irish, who came to be known as the Ascendancy, once stating in an interview that, had the timing been right, he would have been one of the boys hired to collect stray tennis balls at Elizabeth Bowen's estate, Bowen's Court. The stately homes known as "Big Houses", built by these Anglo-Irish families, were both historical fact and the subject of a subgenre of Irish literature embraced by writers as diverse as Somerville and Ross, Elizabeth Bowen, Jennifer Johnston and John Banville. Chapter Four discusses Trevor's own contributions to Big House literature, including the novels *Fools of Fortune*, *The Silence in the Garden* and *The Story of Lucy Gault*, and short stories such as "The News from Ireland". Although Trevor employs some of the conventions of the Big House tradition — declining family, a doomed house, etc. — he also subverts that tradition, compelling his characters to defy expected roles. Trevor's Big House fiction reveals the author's ongoing preoccupation with Ireland's Troubles and its colonial past, and several of these works are thinly veiled allegorical readings of Ireland's history. And although he has denied that he is a political writer, it is clear that Ireland's colonial past and the injustices and inequities it spawned preoccupy him, as does the deplorable tendency of a violent past to repeat itself.

Always concerned with imbalances in power, whether it be a child dominated by an insensitive teacher or a homeless person cast away by a prosperous society, Trevor plumbs the social psychosis generated by colonialism, a psychosis that wounds colonised and coloniser alike. Chapter Five examines the world into which Trevor was born, a world he has described as "poor Protestant" Ireland. Having witnessed in his own lifetime the shrinking power and population of middle-class Protestants in the Republic of Ireland and the new resurgence of Catholic Ireland under Eamon de Valera's leadership, Trevor is acutely aware of the sense of dislocation and loss that that change entailed. Trevor seems to have accepted the shift of power with both equanimity and some regret, recognising, as have many before and since, that de Valera's insistence on Catholic hegemony was both divisive and unrealistic. In Trevor's "poor Protestant" fiction, those characters who cannot adjust to changing times face extinction — not through violence, but through biology: they literally fail to reproduce.

Occasionally taking his exploration of middle-class Protestant Ireland north of the border, Trevor in "Lost Ground" scrutinises the ugly face of religious intransigence, whereby a family sacrifices a son to a violent death because he has shaken their familiar world of Ulster, Union, and anti-Catholicism. Uninterested in judging the Leesons, Trevor instead reveals through them the tragedy wrought by bigotry, fear, and the inability to change.

Chapter Six argues that, despite his sympathy for Irish nationalism, Trevor also explodes both colonial and nationalist icons of Irish women, pointing up the disparities between the mythic Rosaleens and Cathleens and the oppression of real

Irish women. Trevor compels us to "de-colleenise" Ireland, to peel away these reductive images.

Trevor's Irish fiction has taken an increasingly allegorical slant, with Irish history playing itself out on fields as small as a family and as large as the island of Carriglas, where *The Silence in the Garden* is set. But he tweaks expectations, breaking down the myths that have defined and constrained the Irish. In *Fools of Fortune*, a Big House family befriends a disgraced priest and supports Michael Collins; in "Lost Ground", a young man from a militantly Unionist family believes he has visions of a Catholic saint; in "The News from Ireland", an English Protestant governess tells the Catholic servants in a Famine-era Big House the Legend of the True Cross. Chapter Seven discusses Trevor's most sustained allegorical reading of Anglo-Irish relations, *Felicia's Journey*. Employing the machinery of a popular thriller — a suspected serial killer zeroes in on his latest victim — Trevor explodes the English imperialist and Irish nationalist myths that have hobbled Joseph Ambrose Hilditch, English stalker of vulnerable young women, and Felicia, his latest, and only Irish, victim.

Chapter Seven discusses Trevor's most recent collection of stories, *The Hill Bachelors*, which reveals the author's evolving tendency to dissolve confining categories, to reconfigure traditional scenarios. Would-be emigrants, unseduced by better economic opportunities abroad, remain home; despite its daunting loneliness, a man chooses to save a remote family farm from extinction; a Catholic and a Protestant clergyman discover their common ground. Quietly dramatic in the face of stunning social and economic change, these stories urge the importance of resilience, the necessity for imagination.

The final chapter discusses *The Story of Lucy Gault*, Trevor's first Irish novel in eight years. Though the novel's Big House setting recalls such earlier works as *Fools of Fortune* and *The Silence in the Garden*, its understated style only thinly masks the author's bold re-imagining of both a literary tradition and a reconfiguration of his own Irish writing. Reversing expected patterns, playing variations on his earlier Irish fiction, *The Story of Lucy Gault* is the author's boldest, most brilliant allegory of Ireland.

Trevor's resistance of expected categories has perhaps contributed to his relative critical neglect by commentators on Irish literature. His very versatility renders him difficult to "place", or even results in his being incorrectly categorised as Anglo-Irish, when in fact his family roots in Ireland are deep, an ancestor having converted to Protestantism, probably for economic survival, in the wake of the severely repressive Penal Laws. His Irish fiction is wide-ranging, including as its subject matter Dublin, middle-class Protestants, the North, the Big House, the Troubles, the legacy of Ireland's domination by England; yet discussions of any of the above areas often ignore Trevor's contribution.

In fact, Trevor's Irish fiction increasingly calls for his readers to "re-imagine" Ireland as a diverse island. By no means a revisionist in his reading of Irish history, Trevor compassionately acknowledges the tragedies and injustices of the past, yet insists on the dangers of entrapment in that past — the need, as Hugh O'Donnell urges in Brian Friel's *Translations*, to renew the images that define the Irish people.

Chapter One

An Uneasy Dubliner

Although the bulk of William Trevor's Irish fiction is set in provincial Ireland, where he spent his childhood, the author's first Irish novel and several of his short stories are set in Dublin. The author visited Dublin as a child, attended boarding school there, and completed a degree in History at Trinity College in 1950. But his memoirs, *Excursions in the Real World*, and his fiction recall his frequent unhappiness at boarding school, his detachment from his university studies — an indifference he later came to regret — and his perception of Dublin as an alien, sometimes threatening place, particularly for the outsider, a place he never felt at home.

> I have myself remained a visitor in Dublin for a lifetime. Years of schooling there, of university, of being employed there and living there, have not altered that. It is said that once a city is a capital it is everybody's. Natives and visitors stake different claims and offer different perspectives: muddle makes cities what they are. This may be true, but in this present case it doesn't seem entirely so: Dublin belongs to Dubliners.
>
> As a schoolboy, I met them for the first time — sharp-witted, sharp-tongued, sharp in appearance even. The provincial is no match for these wily

> locals; this is their place and still their Pale. "Dublin
> jackeens", you might say in County Cork or County
> Wexford; you kept the expression to yourself in
> O'Connell Street. (*ERW*, 76–7)

The sense of Dublin as alien territory, as a place where the
outsider becomes isolated and victimised, pervades much of
Trevor's Dublin fiction. However, despite his feelings of for-
eignness in the city, Trevor has been a close, intrigued observer of Dubliners, whether he has encountered them on
street corners or at academic gatherings. His first Irish
novel, *Mrs Eckdorf in O'Neill's Hotel* (1969), reflects his fascination with the diverse characters of Dublin as well as the
influence of James Joyce.

It is inevitable that any modern Irish writer dealing with
the Dublin scene must face comparison and come to terms
with James Joyce. Trevor has expressed great admiration for
Joyce, particularly for the short stories in *Dubliners*, preferring
them and *A Portrait of the Artist as a Young Man* to Joyce's later
work. As he stated in an interview with RTE, Joyce "was an
eye-opener" (Ní Anluain, 2000: 227), and *Dubliners*, which so
impressed the sixteen-year-old Trevor when he first read it,
continues to be "important" to him.

Certainly, Joyce's evident influence on Trevor has been
noted by commentators on his fiction. As does Joyce in *Dubliners* and *Ulysses*, Trevor frequently depicts characters
trapped in restrictive, stagnant environments; his characters
and readers likewise undergo Joycean moments of illumination or "epiphanies". Yet though he obviously admires Joyce
and to some extent emulates him, Trevor makes crucial sty-
listic and thematic departures from him. Further, Trevor
writes of Dublin as an outsider, not with the intimacy and
affection, however grudging, of Joyce.

Ivy Eckdorf, an English photographer specialising in cof-
fee-table books, journeys to Dublin to find O'Neill's Hotel

after a casual conversation has convinced her that a dramatic story is waiting to be uncovered there. The novel opens with ludicrous humour that quickly trembles on the verge of tears — a tension that will be sustained for most of the novel. Mrs Eckdorf sees it as her calling to expose the hidden realities of her subjects' lives. She sees herself as a truth-teller, one who does not flinch from examining human misery. But just as the truth can be cruel, Mrs Eckdorf in her pursuit of what she believes to be true is ruthless — and, paradoxically, deceptive: she has no compunction about lying in order to gain people's co-operation, as when she poses as a potential buyer for the down-at-heels hotel owned by the Sinnott family and thus falsely raises hopes that the decaying building will be resurrected.

The lives into which Mrs Eckdorf intrudes herself are not the stuff of high drama but closer to Thoreau's "lives of quiet desperation". O'Neill's Hotel has, unbeknownst to most of the Sinnotts, degenerated into a part-time whorehouse, and one of the many orphans Mrs Sinnott has befriended over the years, Agnes Quin, is now a prostitute; another, Morrissey, practises, among other unsavoury activities, pimping. A third orphan, the pathetic hotel porter O'Shea, clings to the impossible hope that O'Neill's will one day return to its former glory.

Mrs Sinnott's two children, Eugene and Enid, have likewise led disappointed lives. Now in their fifties, both have married unhappily. Eugene, unkempt and too fond of drink and gambling, continues to live in his boyhood room in O'Neill's where he brought his new bride, Philomena, many years before. Now the couple has been separated for 28 years, and Philomena smothers their adult son, Timothy John, with overanxious love. Enid, married to the cold, tight-fisted head of an insurance department, mentally recites recipes in order to block out her husband's boring monologues about his latest moneymaking scheme, and despite

her disappointment in her marital choice, continues to sub-
ordinate her own desires to her domineering husband's.

The emotional centre of all these unhappy lives is Mrs
Sinnott herself. A deaf mute whose very silence encourages
others to confide in her, she recalls the work of another
author Trevor admires, Carson McCullers (Ní Anluain,
2000: 238). Like John Singer in McCullers' *The Heart is a
Lonely Hunter*, Mrs Sinnott's own thoughts remain unshared.
While her visitors have consigned their dreams and fears
and disappointments to her steadily mounting pile of exercise books, she has reminisced about her happy marriage to
a beloved husband, a union brutally terminated when her
husband was shot, apparently while fighting for Irish independence. Yet, unlike Singer, who is too caught up in his
own loneliness and thwarted love to pay much heed to his
visitors' miseries, Mrs Sinnott cares deeply about the troubled lives that fill the exercise books and is haunted by what
she perceives to be her failure to alleviate her companions'
suffering. Mrs Sinnott also recognises that, unlike her visitors, she has always been loved. In sad contrast, they have
failed in or been failed by love. Agnes Quin, though she
wants to leave her life as a prostitute and open a shop, nevertheless has found in prostitution a pathetic substitute for
the love she craves. Morrissey, though physically and morally
repugnant, is likewise blighted by lovelessness. Envious of
those who have friends, he forges his own solitude by his
ineptitude in relating to others.

O'Shea, the hotel porter, likewise leads a solitary existence. Devoted to Mrs Sinnott and unabashedly hostile to
Morrissey, he sees in Mrs Eckdorf a saviour for the sadly de-
teriorated hotel. To his disquietude, she also stirs his sexual
desires, long dormant because of his religion-induced prud-
ishness. Stubbornly clinging to the hope that O'Neill's will one
day again be a prosperous hotel, O'Shea is a sad, gently comic
figure. He is also the most victimised by Mrs Eckdorf in her

ruthless quest for the "secret" of O'Neill's Hotel, for he has trusted in her completely and believed that she will indeed buy the hotel. Even Father Hennessey, who as a priest has dedicated his life to love of God and humanity, has failed in human relationships — and he is painfully aware of the fact.

As we learn almost at the novel's outset, Mrs Eckdorf has led a professionally successful but personally disastrous life. Devoted as a child to her loving father, she is abandoned by him after her parents' divorce. Not only must she endure the trauma of her father's defection, she is also deeply disturbed by her mother's sexual promiscuity. At school, she is shocked when a trusted teacher makes sexual advances to her. After leaving England because it held "'unpleasant associations'", she moved to Germany, where her two subsequent marriages failed. As she confesses to Father Hennessey, neither marriage was consummated; since childhood, sex has had distasteful overtones of sordidness and betrayal for her.

Though Mrs Eckdorf asserts that her own relationships have consistently failed, throughout the novel she insists on the necessity for human connection. To the hapless Englishman she buttonholes on the flight to Ireland, she declares, "'We are all a part of one another, my dear, and we must all know one another better'" (*ME*, 16). Yet both Mrs Eckdorf's profession and her associations with other people seemingly contradict her assertions about charity and compassion: her books have been ruthless scrutinies of human suffering. Mrs Eckdorf pursues her subjects passionately, and often at the cost of great personal discomfort and personal risk, but "It had never not been worth it" (86). And though she believes that her books succeed in bringing people together — the numerous letters she receives attesting to how she has moved her audience convince her that such is the case — we share the disquietude of the Englishman, who says, "'What I honestly think . . . is that no one has the right to go poking about in other people's lives in order to make money, or indeed for any other reason. There's such a thing as privacy"' (16). Father Hennessey, too, is made uneasy.

But the truth is elusive here, for both the Englishman and Father Hennessey seem inclined to avoid unpleasant realities. Yet whereas Mrs Eckdorf's assertion that people should learn to understand each other is compelling, her own motives in exposing painful realities are mixed: work has become an escape from private pain, and her observation of others renders her at times a rather pathetic voyeur — as her first name, Ivy, indicates, she feeds on other people's lives — unable to engage in human contact without her shielding camera. And in fact, for all her assertions of humanity, Mrs Eckdorf exhibits paradoxically insensitive behaviour. The Sicilian villagers, subjects of one of her books, beg her not to expose their priest, who has lost his faith, because they fear Church authorities and even damnation, but she will not be moved: ". . . for it was right, she knew, that the fears and faithfulness of poverty-dogged peasants should be seen and understood on the coffee-tables of the rich" (123). Once in Dublin, she orders a persistent beggar woman to "'Get off to hell'"; when she photographs a man who in hopes of receiving payment relates his family's serious economic predicament, she remains emotionally detached, musing that if poverty ceased to exist so too would her penetrating photographs, for subjects hopeful of remuneration pose more naturally. Mrs Eckdorf does not flinch at lying to get what she wants, nor does she feel uneasy at her intrusion into the Sinnott family's private lives, an intrusion she makes under false pretences.

Mrs Eckdorf's sense of destiny about O'Neill's Hotel proves prophetic: her experiences in Dublin will irrevocably change her life, but will not result in the book she had anticipated. For, to her horror, Mrs Eckdorf realises that the compelling "tragedy" she has sought out was never alluded to by a ship's barman but was instead her own invention. Her world begins to unravel dizzyingly: when Mrs Sinnott, whom she has comes to love, dies, Mrs Eckdorf's behaviour becomes increasingly irrational. Finally, it becomes clear that Dublin will indeed be her destiny: she will live out her days there in a mental asylum.

But Mrs Eckdorf's madness, to quote Emily Dickinson, contains within it "divinest sense". Gregory Schirmer has observed:

> The issue of Mrs Eckdorf's madness, for example, is clouded by the insistently posed question of who is deranged, Mrs Eckdorf or those who dismiss her as mad. . . . Is it simply a question of a woman blinded by fanaticism to the realities of life, a woman who sees forgiveness and compassion where there is neither, or is the world to which she brings her message morally unbalanced because it has become deaf to what she has to say? Trevor's irony constantly keeps the novel moving back and forth between these two poles. (Schirmer, 1990: 42)

In a scene that combines slapstick humour with deadly moral seriousness, Mrs Eckdorf asserts that she must learn to love the seemingly unlovable. Smedley, an insensitive, repugnant man who uses women for sexual gratification, is exactly the sort of man Mrs Eckdorf would fear and despise, yet she must "wash his feet" and thus learn to forgive all those who have injured her. But when she pleads with Fr Hennessey to give her the strength to take such a leap of faith, he fails her, accusing her of self-dramatisation and of inventing a false image of God, and thus he hurls her into despair.

> "You're saying your God's a bearded face," she cried out, "that isn't there at all. You're saying there is nothing but the neediness of the human heart. You're telling me to travail alone. You're telling me

> to clear off and leave you in whatever peace it is you
> know." (229)

Fr Hennessey is neither an insensitive nor an unfeeling man, but he is unimaginative and reluctant to explore the dark places of the soul that Mrs Eckdorf has unearthed.

When Mrs Eckdorf succumbs to the madness that has stalked her throughout the novel, Fr Hennessey visits her regularly — not because he wants to, but because to do otherwise would be in his eyes a betrayal of his priestly vows. By the end of the novel Mrs Eckdorf has slipped into a fantasy world in which O'Neill's flourishes once more and the Sinnott family is happy and prosperous. So lovely and comforting is this imaginary world that Fr Hennessey takes a strange pleasure in his visits.

In reality, life at O'Neill's seems on the decline — except for Agnes Quin, who summons the strength to take a menial job at a convent in order to escape prostitution. Fr Hennessey's is the prevailing consciousness at the novel's close, and his thoughts of Mrs Eckdorf are laced with unwittingly devastating irony: "In the mood that possessed him, the single certainty he felt was that on her behalf there was something he had to render thanks for. For her at least there was a happy ending" (265). In such a bleak setting, it seems that happiness is possible only by detaching oneself completely from reality and building consoling fantasies. Finally, Mrs Eckdorf's intuitive feeling that a tragedy had occurred at O'Neill's is deadly accurate, for this decaying building testifies to the failure of human love.

Joycean touches abound in *Mrs Eckdorf in O'Neill's Hotel.* The use of multiple points of view, simultaneous actions, characters engaged in unheroic quests, and the flashes of outrageous humour recall *Ulysses*; but unlike Stephen Dedalus and Leopold Bloom — the son in search of a father and the father seeking a son, who discover in the Eccles Street kitchen a harmony of sorts — the two prominent male questers in *Mrs Eckdorf* — Morrissey and Smedley, one seeking to ingratiate himself with other men through pimping, the other in search of buyable female flesh — come to no such harmony. Beaten and robbed by the outraged Smedley, Morrissey finds only new fodder for his self-pity and his conviction that people cannot be trusted.

Mrs Eckdorf in O'Neill's Hotel also reveals Trevor's growing preoccupation with Ireland's colonial history. In the late 1960s and early 1970s, escalating unrest in Northern Ireland increasingly spurred Trevor to write in his Irish fiction about the implications of Ireland's historical domination by England. Ivy Eckdorf and Mr Smedley, both English, attempt to exploit Ireland for their own ends, yet each, ironically, is unexpectedly transformed by the encounter. Smedley's search for sexual gratification ends in humiliation, albeit at the hands of Mrs Eckdorf. Mrs Eckdorf believes she can make sense of a city about which she knows nothing by imposing meaning upon it in her glossy book of photographs. When she pries into Mrs Sinnott's exercise books, shamelessly reading the intimate details confided to the elderly woman, she concludes with horror that the secret she had hoped to discover doesn't exist. Unable to face the failure of her quest, she invents a secret: surely Eugene raped Philomena, an action that would explain the ill-fated marriage and Enid's estrangement from her brother. She also mythologises Mrs Sinnott into a saint, even rendering her divine. O'Neill's Hotel to her, then, is not a rundown, part-time whorehouse but rather a holy place where forgiveness is possible.

One of the novel's many ironies is that, despite Mrs Eckdorf's delusions, she hits upon a kind of truth here; but the wondrous happenings she imagines occur in her own life. At O'Neill's Hotel, she discovers uncomfortable truths about her own arrogance and the need to come to terms with her painful past. Her brief encounter with Dublin leaves herself, not Dublin, transformed. As her mental state deteriorates, she hurls her camera into the river, rejecting the art that has been her only secure identity. Significantly, though, some of Mrs Eckdorf's discoveries are well worth hearing, but she meets only incomprehension and rejection. The radical love she ultimately preaches is too undiluted a dose of Christianity for her hearers. Even Fr Hennessey feels repugnance and dismay at Mrs Eckdorf's message.

This first of Trevor's "Irish" novels anticipates the author's later preoccupations in writing about Ireland and the Irish. The use of multiple perspectives underlines, as it does in the later "The News from Ireland", the mutual alienation of the characters. As we have seen, early signs of Trevor's later concern with Ireland's colonial legacy appear in *Mrs Eckdorf* as well.

Mrs Eckdorf in O'Neill's Hotel, though a moving, skilfully written novel, nevertheless betrays Trevor as unsure of his "Irish" voice. The absurd humour and the Dickensian eccentrics who people his early "English" novels such as *The Boarding House* and *The Old Boys* appear in this Dublin-based novel, perhaps revealing the author's uneasiness with his setting, his search to find a way to "write Ireland".

Since the publication of *Mrs Eckdorf in O'Neill's Hotel*, Trevor has only occasionally chosen Dublin as a setting for his fiction. But in this small group of short stories as well, the urban setting is populated by lonely characters searching in vain for love and companionship. And though the Dubliners are free from many of the sexual and social restraints of Trevor's rural and provincial Ireland, they fare no better in forming lasting relationships.

The Irish stories in Trevor's first four collections of short stories — *The Day We Got Drunk on Cake* (1967), *The Ballroom of Romance* (1972), *Angels at the Ritz* (1975), and *Lovers of Their Time* (1978) — for the most part are set in provincial or rural Ireland. Beginning with the 1981 collection *Beyond the Pale*, Trevor chooses Dublin as the setting for a handful of stories — "Downstairs at Fitzgerald's" and "The Time of Year" (*Beyond the Pale*); "Music" and "Two More Gallants" (*The News From Ireland*); "The Third Party" and "In Love With Ariadne" (*Family Sins*); and "A Bit of Business" (*After Rain*). Focusing as they do on trapped, unhappy lives, these stories recall *Dubliners*, and Trevor makes no bones about the Joycean antecedent of "Two More Gallants".

Trevor has often written insightfully about sensitive children trapped in unromantic settings. The children are usually male, living in the kind of small towns where Trevor spent his own childhood. "Downstairs at Fitzgerald's" departs from this pattern, concerning as it does a young girl's gradual comprehension of what her parents' divorce has done to her father's life. In addition, the story takes place in Dublin, not in a provincial setting.

Yet despite its female protagonist and urban setting, "Downstairs at Fitzgerald's" could be at home in one of Trevor's provincial towns: Dublin is not essential to this retrospective tale of the 1940s, when a child is saddened by her father's emotional and economic decline and pained by a schoolmate's suggestion that her stepfather is also her biological father.

The Dublin setting is more apt in "The Time of Year", in which Valerie Upcott leaves her provincial Irish home to study at Trinity College, as Trevor did himself. Like Gretta Conroy in Joyce's "The Dead", she is secretly haunted by the death of the boy she loved, and that tragedy has rendered her a melancholy, detached spectator of Dublin student life. The sorrow of her loss is particularly vivid because the story takes place at Christmas time, the anniversary of her boyfriend's death, and because the swimming outing on which he drowned was her idea, she carries the additional burden of guilt.

Valerie's Dublin, as in Joyce's stories, is a dreary place, her companions shallow and uninspiring. Attending a party at her History professor's house, an event that is not a freely chosen pleasure but rather a command performance, Valerie finds herself in a decidedly Joycean interior, brown being the predominant hue. Haunted by her own mournful thoughts, she observes detachedly the manoeuvrings of her fellow students, none of whom is enjoying Professor Skully's boring party but who fear academic repercussions if they do not attend. To Valerie, their lives seem so uncomplicated, so predetermined.

As she watches her companions, Valerie experiences an uncomfortable epiphany, realising the hollowness of the Skullys' lives (the variant spelling of this familiar Irish name underlines the perception). She senses that both are not fully alive, that both are oddly lacking in humanity: "It was as if . . . they lived together in the dead wood of a relationship, together in this house because it was convenient" (*CS*, 807). This realisation triggers a more personal epiphany, a partial insight fraught with irony.

> She had been wrong to imagine she envied other people their normality and good fortune. She was as she wished to be. She paused in faint moonlight, repeating that to herself and then repeating it again. She did not quite add that that tragedy had made her what she was, that without it she would not possess her reflective introspection, or be sensitive to more than just the time of year. But the thought hovered with her as she moved towards the lights of the house, offering what appeared to be a hint of comfort. (809)

Though Valerie's suffering has perhaps rendered her more perceptive, less willing to be wooed by the shallow lifestyles she encounters in Dublin, she faces a danger similar to that of the Skullys. Guilt and unhappiness have excluded her from "life's feast" (to recall Mr Duffy from "A Painful Case") and the hedging language of the conclusion points up the ambiguities of Valerie's character: she reaches her moment of illumination in "*faint* moonlight"; her several repetitions that "she was as she wished to be" are indicative of doubt; the house lights *appear* to offer a "*hint* of comfort" (emphasis mine). By the end of "The Time of Year" we are not convinced that Valerie will extricate herself from the tragedy of the past.

"Two More Gallants" recalls Joyce's masterly, deeply unpleasant story of Corley, a repugnant young man who exploits the servant girl who loves him, and Lenehan, his toadying, down-at-heels follower. Just as Corley's greed and desire to show off his power over his girlfriend drive him to persuade her to steal a gold coin from her employers, Trevor's counterpart to Corley, Heffernan, is driven by a strong passion: revenge.

The nameless narrator of Trevor's story recalls how Heffernan and FitzPatrick, once nearly inseparable companions, have been estranged for nearly thirty years because of Heffernan's ugly act of vengeance against an elderly professor. Heffernan is a perennial student (probably at Trinity College) because he has been left a bequest that will cease if he leaves school. Now that he is over 30, his continuing presence elicits a mild joke from Professor Flacks — "'I see you are still with us'" — that gravely offends Heffernan's considerable pride and spurs him to take brutal vengeance.

FitzPatrick, like Joyce's Lenehan, is a doglike follower who is less reprehensible than his companion. We recall Lenehan's lonely walk through Dublin, his meagre dinner in a cheap restaurant, and his desire to escape his aimless life. FitzPatrick, like Lenehan, is guilty of moral sloth or *accidie*: both are in a position to prevent evil; neither intervenes.

Heffernan isolates the great passion of Flacks's life — his Joyce scholarship — and ruthlessly sets out to destroy the professor's reputation. He pays an avaricious elderly woman to go along with his fabrication that she knew James Joyce and was the model for the skivvy in "Two Gallants". Fitz-Patrick is suspicious of the story and is also surprised to discover that, unlike the monster of Heffernan's stories, Flacks is gentle and courteous. But FitzPatrick's almost pathological laziness renders him both imperceptive and inactive.

FitzPatrick does not rouse himself to question Heffernan's plans. In fact, the offended student executes a malicious revenge: after the elderly professor delivers a well-received lecture to the Society of the Friends of James Joyce about his exciting findings, Heffernan stands up and reveals the hoax. So repelled is he by this cruelty that FitzPatrick finally acts, rejecting Heffernan's friendly overtures and severing their relationship. Heffernan's act has lasting consequences, for Flacks dies the following year, his humiliation public knowledge. And though Robert Rhodes has asserted that Flacks is "himself hubris-ridden enough not to have penetrated the secret scheme against him" (Rhodes, 1989: 38), the final image of a humiliated old man is more potent than any desire to affix blame to that man's vanity.

The story's ending is disappointingly flat. We do not know enough about the narrator to judge the tone of the final paragraph, and as a result the edge of this story of cruelty is blunted:

> We spoke of his [Flacks's] playful sarcasm and how so vehemently it had offended Heffernan's pride. We marvelled over the love that had caused a girl in a story to steal, and over the miserliness that had persuaded an old woman to be party to a trick. Fitz-Patrick touched upon his own inordinate laziness, finding a place for that also in our cobweb of human frailty. (CS, 1032–3)

Perhaps the narrator's rather indulgent attitude is meant to connect him with the moral inertia of FitzPatrick; perhaps Trevor means to end this story of rankling resentment with a plea for compassion, but the final ambiguity is irritating rather than enlightening. Jim Haughey theorises that Trevor's story, like Joyce's, explores the effects of Ireland's colonial history upon Ireland's men, including their tendency to vent their feelings of powerlessness and frustration by exploiting women, but that ultimately both authors oppose "cultural essentialism" (Haughey, 1995: 365), recognising that Irish identity is complex and should not be defined by such "binary" categories as Catholic and Protestant, nationalist and unionist. But though certainly much of Trevor's Irish fiction grapples with this very issue, "Two More Gallants" does not easily bear such considerable weight.

Like "Two More Gallants", "Music" makes direct allusion to Joyce, for Joyce is one of the protagonist's heroes. Justin Condon's story is told in retrospect: now 33, he has clung for years to his childhood dream of being a world-renowned musician. Through his memories, we discover how crucial childhood experiences have stunted his life.

Perhaps no other contemporary writer has captured as Trevor can the dreariness of middle-class life. Justin, a native of the Dublin suburb of Terenure, is a travelling salesman of ladies' undergarments, a job decidedly at odds with his grandiose dreams of composing a symphony about the legendary Queen Medb. Though Justin's inner life is rich, outwardly he inhabits a world of small-town shopkeepers and the tedious conversations at Mrs Keane's boarding-house, where he has caught the romantic interest of a dentist, Thomasina Mac-Carthy. Through detailed descriptions of the stale odours, the dreary surroundings, and the vulgar conversations that are Justin's daily fare, Trevor heightens our sense of this young man's entrapment.

Justin believes he is simply biding his time: someday, like his heroes, Joyce and Gauguin, he will leave behind his unsatisfying life and escape to the dizzying freedom of artistic exile. Joyce is a particularly resonant presence in his life, for he sees the author as a fellow sufferer of Dublin's dreariness, yet one who made a spectacular escape.

Justin's dreams of a more stimulating life were conceived during childhood, but not at home. His father is a loud, coarse man who never tires of relating the practical jokes of his youth; his hearty jokiness rendered him a popular, successful salesman, and Justin suspects that the customers he has inherited from his father believe that the son is a poor substitute. Justin's mother is a worried, shadowy woman. The family considers him odd because he takes no interest in hurling or betting, preferring to take long, solitary walks.

Justin discovers his emotional home with Aunt Roche, an unmarried woman who befriended him as a child and who comes to view him as her adopted son. With her frequent guest, Father Finn, she encourages Justin's interest in music, and the three of them become a much more intimate and loving family than Justin's own. What Justin does not realise is that Aunt Roche and Fr Finn are in love. Their religious convictions prevent their marrying, but Justin's piano lessons with the priest at Aunt Roche's house become a socially acceptable excuse for the couple to be together. Though they genuinely love Justin, they also exploit him, encouraging him to believe that his musical talent is immense; in fact, they exaggerate his prowess in order to protract his visits.

When Fr Finn is dying, he conveys his tremendous sense of guilt to Aunt Roche and urges her to right the injustice they have been perpetrating for so many years. When Aunt Roche attempts to do so, Justin feverishly tries to forestall the revelation. In a pathetic scene, he blurts out his father's tiresome stories; he knows that once the truth is spoken his fate will be determined.

> For a long time now he had known he could play the
> piano in a tidy, racy way, that possibly he possessed
> no greater gift. It was his longing to walk away from
> his Ford Fiesta, from his parents' house and from Ire-
> land, that made him different from his father, not his
> modest musical aptitude. (*CS*, 1084)

But Aunt Roche will not be deterred: she confesses that she
and Fr Finn exploited Justin's "simplicity". He in turn feels
foolish and ashamed, and with his long-cherished hope vanished, makes a heartbreaking decision: he will become like
his father, a fast-talking salesman with a store of jokes and
probably a shopkeeper mistress; he will marry Thomasina
MacCarthy, whom he does not love, because "such things
happened when you had nothing to keep you going" (1085).

Even in her final confession, Aunt Roche is self-indulgent:
she seems more concerned with assuaging her own guilt
than with the revelation's impact upon Justin. His dreams
were essentially harmless, and perhaps even had he discovered in time that his artistic fantasies were unrealistic, he
might have salvaged enough strength to escape his confining
life. But his bitter discovery that he has been deceived —
and by people he loved and trusted — causes him to despair. He acquiesces to social convention and in so doing
incurs emotional death.

Just as country-bred Valerie of "The Time of Year" discovers in Dublin not a sophisticated urban scene but rather,
shallow, empty lives, Trevor turns the tables in "The Third
Party", in which a wronged husband from provincial Ireland
discovers that his wife's Dublin-bred lover is a naïve, inexpe-
rienced man. In a sense, the story pits the provincial Ireland
of much of Trevor's fiction against the rather bloodless
world of contemporary Dublin.

Fergus Boland has agreed to meet his wife's lover in
Dublin to discuss the trio's future. His twelve-year marriage

has been slowly deteriorating, and he tells himself that if he remains calm Annabella will pass unregretted out of his life. But Boland is at once a shrewd, perceptive and self-deluding man. The lover, Lairdman, is unimpressive: small, priggish, and priestly-looking, his attempts to be "civilised" in such an impossible, highly charged emotional situation at first amuse Boland, then anger him. He cannot help but notice betraying characteristics: Lairdman's hesitation to reach for his wallet when drinks arrive, revelatory of his "meanness"; his praise for the wretched school both men attended; and his pretended ignorance when Boland recalls how the Dublin boy's "uppitiness" caused him to have his head dunked in a toilet bowl.

Boland realises how little Lairdman knows Annabella — and as is typical of Trevor's writing, we are uncertain as to the validity of the character's perceptions: we cannot tell how true are the assessments of this aggrieved husband, for he certainly cannot be objective. Resentment bubbles up in him: "Cuteness was the one thing you could never get away from in Dublin. Cute as weasels they were" (CS, 1144). For complex reasons, Boland thwarts his wife's defection. Knowing that Lairdman wants a family, Boland assures him that Annabella cannot have children — an assertion whose truth is uncertain to the very end of the story — because he senses that the information will cause a rift between them. Travelling home, he recalls the sad deterioration of his marriage, and realises how the childless, Dublin-reared Annabella must have felt trapped in the provincial town that was her husband's home. His thwarting of Annabella's affair seems motivated in part by a lingering affection for her (or at least regret that he has not made her happy); in part by his provincial pride: this smug Dubliner with the telling surname opens old wounds and revives bitter memories, and Boland cannot allow himself to be the loser; and in part by his resentment of his wife's new-found happiness. But to the end of the story, Boland does not fully understand (nor do we) why he has scotched the affair: "Boland remained there for a long time, wondering why he hadn't been able to let Lairdman take her from him" (1149).

In the haunting "In Love With Ariadne", provincial Ireland and Dublin clash once again. Barney Prenderville falls in love with the mysterious Ariadne while he is in Dublin studying medicine. This story too has Joycean touches: Ariadne's surname is Lenehan, as is one of the characters' in "Two Gallants"; she lives on Gogarty Street, perhaps to recall Oliver St John Gogarty, the Irish writer on whom *Ulysses*' Buck Mulligan is based; a minor character is Mrs Joyce. In addition, Trevor reveals an ear for the banal conversation of the boarding house and for the randy slanginess of the medical students. One can imagine Joyce writing a similar story; but Trevor's touch is gentler, more restrained.

Though his mother died when he was small, Barney nevertheless had a happy childhood in a small Irish town. In postwar Dublin, Barney as a young man inhabits two discrete worlds: the companionship of fellow students more concerned with sexual conquest than with their studies; and his lodgings at Mrs Lenehan's house on Gogarty Street, where he becomes enamoured of the quiet, unworldly Ariadne.

Ariadne is an anomaly in this household. Mrs Lenehan is being courted by the unromantic Mr Sheehy, who her shrewd, outspoken mother, Mrs Fennerty, asserts is interested only in her property. The banal conversation at Lenehans' not only contrasts sharply to the dreamy romanticism of Barney's growing infatuation with Ariadne, it also serves as part of the ironic foreshadowing that Trevor employs throughout the story. Like the boy in "Araby", Barney does not see that he is pursuing an impossible romance in a decidedly anti-romantic setting, or that his image of Ariadne is largely a self-deluding fantasy. Charmed by Ariadne's beauty, he questions neither her oddness nor the incongruity of his fantasising about bringing her home to Lisscrea as his wife-to-be at the same time that Medlicott is coaxing a young woman into the back seat of a borrowed car — a scene that ends with the outraged owner flinging the couple's clothes onto the street.

Barney's only date with Ariadne is a chaste Sunday afternoon walk during which they share happy childhood memories — he of life at Lisscrea, she of walks with her father, who died when she was a child. The setting is prophetic: it is late autumn, and the couple walks through mounds of decaying leaves. Like so many of Trevor's characters, Ariadne has been blighted by painful childhood experiences: her father, afraid of arrest after he apparently attempted to molest a child, committed suicide, and Ariadne has so internalised her shame and loss that she is unable to lead a happy life. Like Joyce's Eveline, she flees from a possibly happy future and retreats instead to the secure albeit stultifying world of the familiar.

Barney learns of Ariadne's suffering and flight second-hand: apparently feeling alarmed and ashamed at Barney's interest in her, Ariadne escapes to the convent where she once attended school. Mrs Fennerty not only reveals to him Ariadne's past and her own conviction that her granddaughter will remain in the convent for life, she assures him with uncharacteristic gentleness that "'It would have been no good'" and that Ariadne's defection is not his fault: "'You were the first young man, Barney. You couldn't be held to blame'" (*CS*, 1190).

In recent fiction, Trevor seldom ventures into Dublin: the 1996 collection *After Rain* contains one story exclusively set in Dublin, "A Bit of Business", and "Timothy's Birthday", where Dublin and provincial Ireland again meet. Trevor's most recent collection, *The Hill Bachelors* (2000), contains no Dublin stories.

"Timothy's Birthday", though set only partially in Dublin, again implies that Dublin and the provinces are alien worlds. Timothy, only son of a devoted couple who inhabit a derelict country estate, refuses to attend the ritual celebration of his birthday, sending in his stead his streetwise companion Eddie, a youth whom Timothy's now-deceased lover had picked up on a Dublin street. Eddie, whose own poverty has caused him to keep an eye on the main chance, consumes the birthday meal lovingly prepared by Timothy's mother, steals a silver ornament from the house, and plans not to return to Timothy. Eddie perceives that he has been used to hurt and humiliate Timothy's parents, that he is "rough trade" foreign to their genteel world; he wonders what could have inspired such cruelty. For their part, the parents believe that Timothy resents both their extraordinary devotion to each other and his father's inability to accept Timothy's homosexuality. Odo, Timothy's father, bitterly realises that his son will never reclaim Coolattin, the family estate; the family line will die out. Timothy prefers the restored Georgian flat in Dublin he has inherited from his lover.

Trevor reverses expectations about Dublin and the provinces in this story. Eddie, despite his unsavoury past, evinces more sensitivity and decency than the more genteel, sophisticated Timothy. Despite his petty theft, he refuses to take advantage of Timothy's parents; he is repulsed by the part he has been duped into playing. Ironically, though Timothy evidently views Eddie as unsavoury enough to offend and hurt his parents, Eddie dreams of a respectable life, seeing his arrangement with Timothy as only a temporary means of survival.

"A Bit of Business" recalls *Dubliners* in mood and pattern, following the debased quest of two youthful burglars who take advantage of a Papal visit and burgle houses vacated by the faithful. Their names, Gallagher and Mangan, recall "A Little Cloud" and "Araby"; their day, which begins in

excitement and ends in disappointment, recalls "An Encounter". It is apparent, though, that Trevor's voice dominates
the story. As is so often true in his fiction, mercy appears
serendipitously. When the pair mistakenly enter an occupied
house, they refrain from killing the vulnerable Protestant
man who is housesitting for his Catholic neighbours. Gallagher and Mangan, despite the fact that they know the man
will be able to identify them, take the risk of letting him live,
and they spend the rest of the day in eating, drinking, and
casual sex, finally "wondering if the nerve to kill was something you acquired" (AR, 79).

   Trevor's Dublin is far removed from the contemporary
city of burgeoning construction, traffic-congested streets,
and mobs of people on mobile phones. Smaller, more provincial, his Dublin hearkens back to the 1940s and 1950s,
when Trevor with his Cork background and ""hick accent'"
(Ní Anluain, 2000: 229), endured ridicule and isolation.
Though *Mrs Eckdorf in O'Neill's Hotel* is Trevor's first "Irish"
novel, it is his only *Dublin* novel, and the paucity of Dublin-
set short stories indicates Trevor's liberation from two potent influences: Joyce and his city. Over a decade ago, Gregory Schirmer observed of Trevor and Joyce that "there is
evidence that Trevor has come to some kind of terms with
this powerful ghost" (1990, 136). Trevor has increasingly
extricated himself from Joyce and from Dublin, finding his
own voice as a "poor Irish Protestant" whose inspiration is
the provincial Ireland he knows perhaps as intimately as
Joyce knew Dublin.

Chapter Two

High Hopes and Low Ceilings: Provincial Ireland

In the more than thirty years that William Trevor has been writing Irish fiction, the landscape to which he often returns is the provincial Ireland in which he spent his childhood — small towns and farms housing constricted lives of limited opportunity. Dolores MacKenna notes that these are the places that comprise a now-familiar "Trevor's Ireland": it is "a bleak place where people endure life rather than live it; a place of loneliness, frustration, and undramatic suffering" (1999, 139). Trevor's provincial Irish cling to the comforting fantasies afforded by the local cinema, escapist fiction and daydreams.

This Ireland is bounded by neither gender nor religion, for men and women, Protestant and Catholic, find themselves in similar constraints. Nor is it time-specific: common challenges face characters from the 1940s and the 1990s. Though technology and culture may change, opportunities for escape remain limited, lending Trevor's Ireland a peculiar timelessness. Religion's psychological grip upon the Irish may have diminished; economic hardship may have released its stranglehold; yet even in the provincial stories with contemporary settings, characters are often incapable of extricating themselves from stultifying lives.

Though it may be arbitrary to isolate Trevor's provincial fiction into a separate category, considering that setting's pervasiveness throughout his Irish fiction, it is useful to examine a sampling of it to trace not only its continued freshness but also the subtle changes it undergoes.

Much of Trevor's provincial fiction considers how limited opportunity, religious pressure, and economic considerations warp sexuality, love and marriage. Characters enter into loveless marriages of convenience, decisions that often exacerbate rather than alleviate their loneliness.

In one of Trevor's earliest but perhaps most famous Irish stories, "The Ballroom of Romance" (title story of a 1972 collection), the ironically named Bridie is compelled by economic necessity and family loyalty to live on a remote farm with her father, who is unable to maintain the land because he has had a leg amputated. Unlike Edna O'Brien's often brutal and drunken fathers, Bridie's father is kindly, and acutely aware of the burdensome life his daughter leads, yet realises that he could not survive without her.

Bridie's only escape from the drudgery of the farm is the Ballroom of Romance, a shabby dance-hall where she spends her Saturday nights listening to romantic music and dreaming of marriage. But just as the dance-hall's glamour is illusory — a trick of dimmed lights and soft music — so too is its intimation that a more romantic life is possible in this desolate spot. The dance-hall's resident musicians, the Romantic Jazz Band, are middle-aged men, "amateur performers who were employed otherwise by the tinned-meat factory, the Electricity Supply Board, and the County Council" (*CS*, 191), and Trevor punctuates the story with references to romantic songs of the past to contrast with the sad reality of the dancers' lives.

Bridie, now 36, gradually lowers her sights when looking for a husband. After a youthful infatuation with a boy who eventually married a town girl and emigrated to England,

Bridie both resigns herself to fate and clings to hope: "If you couldn't have love, the next best thing was surely a decent man" (196). She fixes her hopes on Dano Ryan, the band's drummer, thinking he will be a good companion who will share the farm labour. But Dano is lost to Bridie as well, having attracted his widowed landlady with his steadiness and his kindness to her disabled son. Bridie discovers that she can entertain plans that would have been inconceivable years before: marriage to Bowser Egan, one of the area's perennial bachelors, men usually dismissed as "wedded already, to stout and whiskey and laziness, to three old mothers somewhere up in the hills" (194).

Bridie's moment of revelation is emotionally costly: fearing that she has become a figure of ridicule in her pursuit of Dano, she decides not to return to the dance-hall, her only source of pleasure. Without mawkishness and with respect for Bridie's stoicism and lack of self-pity, Trevor painfully exposes the bleakness of Irish rural life. There are no villains in this story, but simply characters who have no choices, who bravely endure in the face of disappointment. Though the reader is well aware that Bridie has been deluding herself for years — a fact underlined by Trevor's narrative strategy of juxtaposing a frank omniscient voice against Bridie's modest fantasies — what might in other hands have been a savage exposure of a narrow life becomes a gentle elegy.

Dolores Mullally in "The Property of Colette Nervi" settles for an unromantic marriage because she has no other prospects. Though published in the 1986 collection *The News From Ireland*, the story is set in 1968. Crippled by polio, Dolores spends most of her days assisting her mother in their shop and re-reading her late father's Wild West novels. Because her experience is limited and the realities of her life colourless, Dolores invents a romantic template by fusing the Wild West novels and her memory of the film *From Here to Eternity*, drawing analogies from these unreal worlds to define the mundane reality of her own. The result is both comic and touching: when a French couple comes to view the standing stones that are the only local tourist attraction, Dolores spies their passionate kiss and thinks it is "like in *Travellin' Saddles* when Big Daunty found his Indian love and both of them went into a swoon, lost to the world" (*CS*, 955). Later, worried that her admittedly unprepossessing suitor, Henry Garvey, will reconsider his decision to marry a woman with a shrivelled leg, Dolores imagines him as a departing cowboy, albeit riding a bicycle.

Whereas Bridie abandons her romantic illusions and faces the reality of her life, Dolores seems to find her fantasised world of westerns, films, and French tourists more real than her actual life. On the day of her wedding to Henry Garvey, she thinks not of her future with her new husband but of the French couple and *From Here to Eternity*. Believing herself fortunate to have attracted any man, Dolores ignores Henry's laziness and dishonesty — he has given her a necklace stolen from Colette Nervi, one of the French tourists — and fashions her dreary world into a romantic illusion. The marriage is in fact pragmatic: Henry can assist the disabled Dolores; he in turn will enjoy a comfortable home and perhaps persuade his new mother-in-law to buy him a car.

In other stories, couples are pressured into marriage to satisfy social convention: in "Teresa's Wedding" (*Angels at the Ritz*, 1975), "Honeymoon in Tramore" (*Family Sins*, 1990), and "The Potato Dealer" (*After Rain*, 1996), the brides are pregnant. In the bleak "Teresa's Wedding", Trevor employs a consistently deflationary technique, undermining traditional expectations about weddings and piercing clichés. In contradiction to Fr Hogan's breezy bromides about the "happy pair" is our knowledge that he compelled Artie Cornish to marry the pregnant Teresa and that the marriages of Teresa's sisters, at which he presided and at which he undoubtedly spouted the same clichés, have both turned out badly. Agnes, thinking of her own disappointing choices, observes of the newlyweds, "'Sickens you . . . she's only a kid, marrying a goop like that. She'll be stuck in this dump of a town forever'" (*CS*, 432).

Worst of all, one of the groom's friends boasts that he previously had a sexual relationship with Teresa, causing Artie to question the unborn child's paternity. Teresa's reaction is heartbreaking: "It didn't matter: it was only to be expected that a man you didn't love and who didn't love you would ask a question like that at your wedding celebration" (437).

In "Honeymoon in Tramore", set in 1948, Trevor shifts some of the sympathy from a pregnant bride to her misled groom. Davy Toome marries the pregnant Kitty even though he is well aware that he is not the father of her child. In fact, he has never had sexual relations with her. As in "Teresa's Wedding", romantic illusions are assaulted on all sides by gritty realities: the boarding-house bedroom smells of flies; Kitty relishes the black pudding that Davy finds loathsome; their wedding night begins with watching a motorcycle daredevil and ends with Kitty falling into a drunken sleep, their marriage unconsummated.

Both partners in this marriage are pitiable. Davy, a hired hand on Kitty's family's farm, has long admired her from afar but thought her unattainable. Kitty still loves the father of her child, but he will not marry her, and faced with the threats of social ostracism and the belief that an abortion would result in eternal damnation, she settles for marriage to Davy, who intends to exercise his marital "rights".

Though Davy Toome thinks about the fact that marrying Kitty will improve his financial status, his main motivation is his affection for her. In the more contemporary "The Potato Dealer", characters likewise marry for convenience, but in a changed Ireland their choices are less constrained and more disturbing. Marriage in "The Potato Dealer" is strictly a finan-

cial deal for the bridegroom; for the bride, it is a guarantee
that she will not have to make unwanted changes in her life.

Ellie Larrissey, pregnant by a priest she continues to
love, is pitiable but not so powerless as Teresa and Kitty.
Since the death of her father many years previously, Ellie and
her mother have been financially dependent on her mean-
spirited uncle, who obviously considers them a burden despite their considerable labour on his farm. When he learns
of Ellie's pregnancy, the uncle first urges abortion, despite
his Catholicism. Because Ellie loves the father of her child
despite the impossibility of a long-term relationship with
him, she refuses. And as bleak as life on the farm can be,
with a joyless, bitter uncle and a censorious mother, Ellie
does not want to chance life elsewhere.

Just as changed times render abortion an option for Ellie,
unmarried pregnancy no longer carries the severe social
stigma evident in the earlier stories. For Ellie's uncle and
mother, personal pride seems more pressing than social reality: they cannot tolerate the possibility that neighbours will
gossip. To preserve that pride, the uncle concocts a monstrous deal: Ellie will marry Mulreavy, the potato dealer,
who will be lured by financial gain: the uncle in essence buys
a father for the child — using the compensation money
Ellie's mother received when her husband was killed in an
accident. Mulreavy, known as a sharp dealer, will one day
own the farm; he considers that his ageing lorry will make
potato dealing impossible in the not-too-distant future. The
uncle in his turn gains a man to help work the farm.

What might have been a predictable story about a victimised woman and a mercenary man takes an unexpected
turn, however: Mulreavy becomes emotionally attached to
Ellie's child, who loves him as her father, not realising the
truth. In this loveless, unconsummated marriage, Mulreavy
reveals unsuspected depths, treating Ellie kindly and enjoying
the child's company. Despite the romantic Ellie's thwarted

life and ongoing love for the priest, however, she is finally less pitiable than her husband.

Truth and its telling or concealment are common concerns in Trevor's fiction; "The Potato Dealer" is no exception, for Ellie becomes obsessed with telling her child the truth about her paternity. Her motivation is complicated: she wants the child to know that she was conceived in love; she believes that she is living a lie, and that her child is living a lie. But as much as we sympathise with Ellie and regret her disappointed life, her revelation, though it may unburden her soul, wounds Mulreavy. The truth about Ellie's pregnancy circulates, and Mulreavy is humiliated that people now know the true circumstances of his marriage: that he was not the father of the child but rather a convenient means of preserving family pride. By the end of the story, Mulreavy has acquired a touching dignity. He and the child still love each other; he comes to accept Ellie's assertion that the truth had to be told. Ellie's final observation bespeaks the sadness of this ill-suited couple:

> She mended his clothes, she kept them clean. She assisted him in the fields, she made his bed. In all the time she'd known him she had never wondered about him. (*AR*, 147)

Trevor does not limit pragmatic marriages to the young, however. Widowed Norah O'Neill in "Bodily Secrets" (*The News from Ireland*) decides at age 59 to marry a man she does not love and whose homosexuality will rule out sexual intimacy. Oddly enough, this sad compromise benefits both Norah and her new husband, Basil Agnew.

Norah is driven by multiple motives in her pursuit of Agnew. Her unsentimental, ambitious son has decided to close her late husband's failing factory, so after seventeen years of service, Agnew, the manager, will be unemployed. She is able to offer him financial security; he in turn could make her roomy house less lonely. Defying local gossip about Agnew's private life and her son's angry objection that she is marrying beneath her, that Agnew is after her money, Norah sticks by her decision.

It is not until near the end of the story that we realise that Norah was before their marriage fully aware of Basil's homosexuality, his furtive, shame-filled trips to Dublin in search of companionship, and his subsequent heavy drinking. Though her decision to marry him anyway is bewildering, we discover that Norah has a secret of her own. Once a beautiful woman, she now believes that pregnancy, indulgence in sweets and alcohol, and passing years have shattered that beauty, "a loss she found it hard to bear. She was haunted by herself, by the beauty that had been there in a hotel in Bray [site of her honeymoon]" (CS, 1024).

Despite their mutual loneliness, despite their heavy drinking, each partner gains something from the union. In a setting that views homosexuality as shameful and aberrant, Basil achieves a superficial respectability; Norah ensures that she will never again have to expose a body that she no longer believes desirable. Their compromise offers security of a sort, but no joy.

In "The Piano Tuner's Wives", the happiness of a provincial marriage is diminished not by social convention or religion, but by the bride's inability to extricate herself from the past. Belle, who has loved the blind piano tuner Owen Dromgould since she was a young woman, marries him when she is 59, after his first wife, Violet, has died. Because the trio live in a small community, Belle is aware that her neighbours know she is Owen's second choice — as one comments, "'Well, she got the ruins of him anyway'" (AR, 1).

Violet had enhanced Owen's life by becoming, in effect, his eyes. Refusing to see his blindness as an obstacle, she enabled him to earn a living by driving him to tune pianos and to play the violin at pubs and dances. By providing him with painstaking descriptions of the people and places they visited, Violet opened up a new world to her husband.

Belle's inability to extricate herself from the memory of Violet casts a shadow over her new marriage. Long admired for her beauty, she mourns the fact that her husband can neither see her nor realise that Violet was unattractive. And when small gestures such as replacing the linoleum and acquiring a pet dog fail to exorcise Violet's memory from the couple's home, Belle indulges in a pathetic effort to banish Violet from Owen's mind by deliberately undermining Owen's memories. She contradicts Violet's descriptions of Owen's customers and their homes, desperately attempting to dislodge the legacy of his first wife.

Owen, who, like so many unsighted characters in literature, lacks physical vision but sees deeply into the labyrinth of the human heart, out of love for Belle does not divulge his awareness of her deceit. Neither judging nor blaming his second wife, he concludes that "Belle would win in the end because the living always do. And that seemed fair also, since Violet had won in the beginning and had had the better years" (15). Because of her own deep insecurity Belle is unable to live happily, so busy is she nursing past hurts.

The confinements of provincial Ireland are not limited to the married, however. Just as Joyce demonstrated that Dublin's paralysis began at an early age, Trevor's provincial Irish children are often sensitive souls struggling to overcome repressive or sometimes cruel environments. But unlike Joyce, Edna O'Brien or Frank O'Connor, who have written so movingly about trapped children growing up Catholic in Ireland, Trevor creates children both Catholic and Protestant. Inevitably, the children are scarred by the realisation that the adults they depend on are sometimes hypocritical, sometimes profoundly flawed; in a few stories, such realisations are so damaging that the child grows up a blighted adult incapable of finding happiness in human relationships.

One of the earliest of Trevor's stories of Irish children is also one of his most chilling. "Miss Smith", though not overtly an Irish story, has been described as such by its author (*DP*, 5). James Machen, a sensitive, gentle child, attempts unsuccessfully to please his demanding teacher. Her thoughtless jibes at his ineptitude isolate him from his classmates, and even after she marries and leaves teaching, James is not free from her — as the narrator comments wryly, ". . . Miss Smith, who at first found marriage rather boring, visited the school quite regularly" (*CS*, 134). To her husband, she declares her aversion to James: "'. . . like a weasel wearing glasses. He quite gives me the creeps'" (135).

James senses Miss Smith's revulsion and prays for understanding. Finally he discovers what he believes will be a solution: for a month he picks flowers — sometimes from other people's gardens — and secretly leaves them at Miss Smith's home. The desired result of winning her approval is thwarted, because, angry at his theft, she reprimands him and exposes him to the rest of the town, including his parents. He cannot understand her displeasure — or her past cruelty.

Despite his experience with Miss Smith, James continues to believe adults hold the answer to his dilemma. After posing a hypothetical question to the man who cuts his family's lawn, he is informed that hurt can be mitigated by reciprocal hurt, that everyone, no matter how much bigger, has a "weak spot" — for instance, "'My little daughter's smaller than you. If you hurt her, you'd be hurting me. It'd be the same, you see'" (136). This careless reply initiates disaster. First James causes marital tension and self-doubt for Miss Smith by secretly endangering her child's life — putting glass beads in his pram, etc. She is driven nearly distracted with feelings of failure, and both she and her husband begin to question whether she is a fit mother. Her husband even comes to believe she may be trying deliberately to kill the child.

James perhaps does not fully realise the aptness of his revenge: he gnaws away at the self-confidence of the woman who destroyed his sense of self-worth: she begins to wonder if indeed she wishes harm to her own child. But James's final revenge is appalling and reveals how childhood injury has festered into psychosis. It seems that James has taken the lawnman's advice literally, and murdered Miss Smith's child (141).

"Miss Smith", with its shocking, extreme plot, lacks the subtlety of Trevor's most recent fiction, but it emphasises chillingly the theme that informs many of Trevor's stories about children: the harm that careless — or in Miss Smith's case, callous — adults can cause to vulnerable children.

Though they do not all end in murder or madness, the majority of Trevor's Irish stories about children trace the effects of dull, repressive environments — usually provincial towns — and insensitive adults upon sensitive children. Usually the children are male; often they are unnamed; and many of them are children during the years of Trevor's own youth. "An Evening with John Joe Dempsey", "A Choice of Butchers" (*The Ballroom of Romance*), and "Mr McNamara" (*Angels at the Ritz*), leave the reader to speculate about the future of disillusioned children, whereas "The Death of Peggy Morrissey" (*The Distant Past*), "The Raising of Elvira Tremlett" (*Lovers of Their Time*), and the short novel *Nights at the Alexandra* leave us in no doubt about how miserable children become blighted adults.

John Joe Dempsey lives with his widowed mother in a provincial Irish town. Neither a scholar nor an athlete, John Joe has few companions and indeed is frequently reprimanded by his teacher, Brother Leahy, for slow-wittedness. In fact, adolescent John Joe is really indulging in hilarious sexual fantasies about the town's more corpulent married women. John Joe's sexual curiosity is further piqued by his conversations with the mentally deficient dwarf Quigley, who boasts he has witnessed sexual acts between virtually every married couple in the town. John Joe's association with Quigley is generally frowned upon, and by the story's end his mother has exacted a promise that he will no longer associate with the older man. Yet by the time John Joe makes the promise, he has experienced a painful epiphany about adult life.

On John Joe's fifteenth birthday, Mr Lynch, a man respected in the town for his devotion to his elderly mother, takes it upon himself to initiate the fatherless boy into adulthood. He does so by getting the boy tipsy on stout, giving him cigarettes, and leading him to believe he is prepared to recount a titillating story about his meeting with a "glory girl" in Piccadilly Circus during the Second World War. The exchange is hilarious and revelatory: as John Joe presses Lynch for salacious details, he is disappointed: at the crucial moment, Lynch had a vision of his mother's statue of the Virgin Mary. John Joe, who had been anticipating a lurid sexual story, realises to his disappointment that the "glory girl" was only to get his attention so that Lynch could lecture him on the evils of "dirty" women.

John Joe begins to see beyond Mr Lynch's socially acceptable façade. He believes Lynch joined the British Army in an unsuccessful attempt to escape his domineering mother; now Lynch spends his evenings getting drunk. John Joe also realises that he might one day become like Lynch: unmarried, living with his possessive mother, concealing his true nature.

John Joe's realisation at the story's end implies that adulthood means acquiescing to a complex set of social hypocrisies. He is told to avoid Quigley, whose eccentricity and sexual prurience render him a dubious companion for a young man; but John Joe comes to believe that Quigley voices the same desires that the more repressed and respectable townspeople keep carefully hidden.

Despite these realisations, John Joe at the story's bleak conclusion admits to himself that he will submit to his mother and to social convention: a job at the sawmill awaits him, and it will be easy to discourage Quigley's companionship. But John Joe is still a boy, and his revelation is incomplete; a fuller awareness is left for the reader. For as John Joe sinks into his bed revelling in the privacy and free fantasising his solitude allows him, we are impressed with an image of living death. This boy, enclosed in his iron bed, has already begun to slip into a long and lingering spiritual paralysis.

The children in "A Choice of Butchers" and "Mr McNamara" suffer at the hands of the adults they have trusted. In "A Choice of Butchers", the first-person narrator recalls a disillusioning experience that occurred when he was seven. This child, like so many of Trevor's children, feels out of place in his family. His parents had already raised several children when he was born and, although he says, ". . . I didn't feel then, not yet, that my parents had given so much to them that there wasn't a lot left to give me" (CS, 302), he feels his father's detachment and his mother's weariness. When his father hires Mr Dukelow to be an assistant in his butcher shop, the child discovers the sort of affection and interest that his parents have not shown him. But Mr Dukelow's gentility, skill, and consideration bring about his dismissal: the boy's loutish, coarse father feels too keenly that in comparison to Dukelow he is decidedly inferior.

The contrast between the two men is so pointed that even the young child perceives it. Whereas the boy's father is large, loud, and has maimed his hands through his clumsy butchering, Mr Dukelow is small and slender, and his delicate hands are skilled in the meat-cutting business. Dukelow also introduces a new courtesy and gentleness into the boy's home, and the child discovers a surrogate parent who shares his troubles, plays games with him, and tells him stories. In contrast to the boy's father, who disturbs the child by flirting openly with the family maid in his wife's presence, Mr Dukelow is respectful and gentle to the two women. So taken is the boy with his new friend that he amends his earlier aversion to inheriting his father's trade: "It wasn't until I saw Mr Dukelow going about the business in his stylish way that I began to say to the women that I might be a butcher one day. Mr Dukelow didn't make me feel that he was cutting up dead animals at all: Mr Dukelow made it all seem civilised" (311).

Though the boy's father is bluff and insensitive, he is no fool; he also genuinely loves his son and realises that he himself compares unfavourably to Mr Dukelow. Threatened by his own inadequacy, he dismisses Dukelow, yet makes it seem as though his employee has freely chosen to leave. The story's ending is poignant: we pity the father even as we deplore his unkindness; but most of all we sympathise with the child, who has lost a beloved friend. He sees through his father's drunken blustering and imagines how different all their lives would be if it were his father who was going away: surely his gentle mother would be more happily married to Dukelow, who would never humiliate her by kissing Bridget; surely they would together be a harmonious family. The now-adult narrator can perceive the hurt pride and the jealousy behind his father's brutal behaviour, but the story ends with a sobbing seven-year-old being borne off to bed, bereft of someone he loved and bewildered at the cruelty of adults.

The family in "Mr McNamara" is more harmonious and affectionate, but the father's predominant colour, brown, is a Joycean foreshadowing, for beneath the surface harmony lurks a distressing secret. The narrator, recalling his thirteenth year, describes how his family, Ascendancy on the descent, lived during the Second World War. Their father's grain business takes him regularly to Dublin, and he returns with vivid stories of his drinking companion, Mr McNamara. Mr McNamara's presence is deeply felt in the household: mother and children are well-acquainted with his religious open-mindedness (he is a Catholic, unlike them), the details of his family life, his opinions on Ireland's place in the war, his admiration for the English. Gifts of chocolate and biscuits arrive for the children, as does the boy's most cherished birthday present, a brass dragon encrusted with glass jewels, and his little sister's belief that the trinket is made of gold, emeralds, and rubies foreshadows the story's bitter revelation.

The father dies suddenly on the boy's birthday, and in loneliness and curiosity he seeks out Fleming's Hotel, where his father and the now-legendary Mr McNamara used to meet. To his shock, he discovers that "Mr" McNamara is a woman. Wanting to reveal the secret because "the truth was neat and without hypocrisy", he instead keeps silent, and the now-adult narrator, who like the narrator in "A Choice of Butchers" learns in time to understand his father, at thirteen feels only bitterness and resentment.

In two unusual stories, children's unhappiness and their maladjustment to unsympathetic environments prove so severe that the characters withdraw completely from reality. In both stories, there is a strong suggestion of the supernatural, but as in the best "ghost" stories, the apparitions may in fact be signs of the characters' psychological disturbance.

The narrator of "The Death of Peggy Meehan" (first published as "The Death of Peggy Morrissey") begins his story in 1936, when he was seven. The only child of ageing parents, he lives a life circumscribed by their caution, piety, and their reluctance to let him associate with other children. In a notable touch of Trevor's wry humour, the mother's reason for forbidding everything from movies to walks in the country is her irrational fear that the boy will pick up fleas. Faced with so many restrictions, the boy retreats into a world of fantasy in which he defies authority and mocks the proprieties he is so firmly urged to respect.

Though the narrator relates his story matter-of-factly, we get a poignant sense of how lonely and constrained his childhood must have been. Even his summer vacations are odd excursions for a child: July fortnights at his Aunt Isabella's boarding-house, a gloomy place thick with religious artefacts and inhabited exclusively by priests. In fact, his Aunt Isabella so venerates priests that they become the sole topic of conversation, though several of the priests in this house seem pathetic: alcoholic, tubercular, unsuccessful. Yet even as a child the narrator realises that his parents would be delighted if he were to become a priest someday.

A crisis in the child's life occurs when he is left in the care of young Father Parsloe. The afternoon is one of dizzying freedom — all previously forbidden pleasures are indulged in, from going to the movies to gorging on sweets. As in many of Trevor's stories, the movies exercise great fascination for those who lead colourless or unhappy lives: here the boy is transformed by a film he can neither understand nor forget:

> It was about grown-ups kissing one another, and about an earthquake, and then a motor-car accident in which a woman who'd been kissed a lot got killed. The man who'd kissed her was married to another woman, and when the film ended he was sitting in a room with his wife, looking at her. She kept saying it was all right. (394)

Though the boy has enjoyed himself immensely, his parents disapprove mightily, his father pronouncing the film "wasn't suitable for a child", his mother inspecting his clothes for fleas. Sleepless that night, he imagines a romantic fantasy involving two pretty girls from school, Claire, and Peggy Meehan. The fantasy is a reworking of the film, a romantic triangle resolved by death: "I wanted to love one of them, like the people had loved in the film. I wanted to kiss one and be with one, just the two of us" (396). The child's inability to choose between the two is settled by his imagining

Peggy Meehan's being accidentally killed in an automobile mishap, thus freeing him to be in love with Claire.

At first, such fantasising seems harmless, but when Peggy Meehan does indeed die — albeit of diphtheria — the child becomes tormented by guilt, believing that his thinking her dead in fact caused her to die. So pronounced do these feelings become that he begins to see Peggy, a vision that remains with him for the rest of his life. Though the adult narrator vows that "It was a childish fear, a superstition that occurring to an adult would cause only a shiver of horror" (397), the child is troubled by memories of how he had secretly ridiculed his parents and their religion, fantasised about being a criminal. "I was possessed and evil; the nuns had told us about people being like that" (397). Saddest of all, he must suffer silently: Father Parsloe has become preoccupied with his own problems, and the child has no other confidant.

The vision recurs as the child grows up: Peggy matures with him, and in his eyes, "I was possessed of the Devil, she came herself from God" (398). He is haunted by religious guilt, emotionally estranged from his family, and eventually grows up to be an eccentric, solitary man. Just as he had led a double life as a child, as an adult he observes the proprieties — going to church, receiving the sacraments, working in his father's former office — but secretly he indulges in sexual fantasies about Peggy, and is viewed by the townspeople as a man rendered odd by a "cloistered upbringing".

> All I know is that she is more real for me than anything else in this seaside town or beyond it. I live for her, living hopelessly, for I know I can never possess her as I wish to. I have a carnal desire for a shadow, which in turn is His mockery of me: His fitting punishment for my wickedest thought of all. (399)

Far more frightening than any supernatural explanation of Peggy Meehan is the fact that this child could be so warped and twisted by years of solitude and religious guilt, by parents more dutiful than affectionate. "The Death of Peggy Meehan" remains one of Trevor's most disturbing stories.

The narrator in "The Raising of Elvira Tremlett" is also out of place in his family. Pronounced "slow as a dying snail" by one of his teachers, he is the only child in his family whose future does not seem predetermined: his father has already decided that his brothers will inherit the family garage business, his "plain" sister, Effie, will become a bookkeeper, and that pretty Kitty will undoubtedly marry. Like the father in "A Choice of Butchers", this narrator's father is loud, large, and uncouth, and the boy is just as uncomfortable with him and his trade as was the child in the earlier story.

> The garage was a kind of hell, its awful earth floor made black with sump oil, its huge indelicate vices, the chill of cast iron, the grunting of my father and my uncle as they heaved an engine out of a tractor, the astringent smell of petrol. It was there that my silence, my dumbness almost, must have begun. (CS, 649)

The narrator's mode of escape is a departure into an imaginary world inhabited by Elvira Tremlett, whose quietness, as he says, is a welcome contrast to his noisy home, whose sympathy relieves the ridicule and bewilderment with which his family treats him. Not until later do we learn with a *frisson* of unease that Elvira Tremlett was an English girl who died in the boy's Munster town in 1873.

The narrator reveals that not only does Elvira provide beauty and tenderness in his unhappy world, she also unveils to him the secret of his estrangement from his family: through her he comes to believe that he is really his Uncle Jack's son, hence the uncle's shame, his father's periodic outbursts of anger, and the family's general uneasiness with him. But when the narrator speaks aloud to Elvira in the family's presence, he begins a downward spiral of madness

and suffering: Elvira now appears to him as an aged, debilitated woman, blaming him for disturbing her rest. "Yet she
was no ghost. She was a figment of my imagination, drawn
from her dull grey tablet by my interest. She existed within
me, I told myself, but it wasn't a help" (657). The narrator is
eventually judged mentally incompetent and taken to an asylum. In his own judgement, "All I had done was to talk to a
figment. All I'd done was to pretend, as they had" (657).

In fact, in the asylum the narrator discovers a peace that
his home did not offer him. He believes, though his visions
have ceased, that "She brought me here so that I could live
in peace . . . " (658), and that Elvira herself once resided in
the asylum, eventually dying there.

As in "The Death of Peggy Meehan", the rational explanation is far more terrifying than any ghost story. The narrator's suspicions about his origins seem plausible, as does the
family's uneasiness with the situation. But as in the previous
story, a highly sensitive, strongly imaginative child cannot
withstand life in a stultifying, unaffectionate family and slips
into a sort of madness.

In the novella *Nights at the Alexandra*, an expansion of an
earlier short story, "Frau Messinger", a child is likewise alienated from his family and finds diversion with an idealised
woman; but in this story, the supernatural element is missing,
the boy's mode of coping with unhappiness less extreme.

Harry, now 58, recalls the year when he was fifteen. Son
of a Protestant lumberyard owner in a humdrum provincial
town, Harry dreads the prospect of working in his father's
timber business. Life at Reverend Wauchope's rectory,
where Harry boards while attending grammar school, is uninspiring as well. When Harry meets Frau Messinger, a beautiful young Englishwoman married to an ageing German, he
discovers an escape from his dull existence. The Messingers
have been displaced by the Second World War, and neutral
Ireland seems the only viable refuge, since each would be

viewed as an enemy in the other's homeland. Frau Messinger, who finds Harry a sympathetic listener, fascinates him with stories of her life in Europe, and he becomes a regular visitor at Cloverhill, the estate her husband is reclaiming for her.

The Messingers offer Harry an alternative to the vulgarities of home and rectory: in fact, they introduce an element of magic into this grey provincial town. Herr Messinger undertakes the building of an elegant cinema, named "The Alexandra" for his wife, as a gift of love to her; she wishes to bring happiness to the people of the town where they have found political asylum. Herr Messinger promises employment for Harry, thus rescuing him from the timberyard. But while the cinema is under construction, Harry realises that Frau Messinger is dying, and the realisation renders him oblivious to his parents' anger — his mother's because she distrusts Frau Messinger's interest in him, his father's because the son wants nothing to do with the timberyard.

When the Alexandra finally opens, it works a curious magic on the town, transforming mundaneness into romance:

> Shoulders slumped, heads touched, eyes were lost in concentration. My brothers did not snigger in the Alexandra, my father, had he ever gone there, would have at last been silenced. Often I imagined the tetchiness of the Reverend Wauchope softening beneath a weight of wonder, and the sour disposition of his wife lifted from her as she watched *All This and Heaven Too*. (NA, 74)

Herr Messinger, whose own private sorrows include not only the imminent death of his wife but also worries about family still in Germany, in his selfless act of love brings hope and romance to others. Undoubtedly Harry's vision of the Alexandra's transforming power is idealised, as is his view of Frau Messinger, but what Trevor seems to be suggesting is

how love and beauty can metamorphose even the most dis-
pirited and earthbound.

But after Frau Messinger's death her husband leaves Cloverhill, and Harry becomes caretaker of the boarded-up
house and eventually the proprietor of the Alexandra. And
as in many of Trevor's stories about children, the obsessions
of youth stymie the adult: Harry, like many of Trevor's
young people, grows up to be a solitary, eccentric man:
when interest in the movies dwindles, he refuses to sell the
Alexandra, and prefers to leave the building vacant. But
whereas many of the child characters are injured by callous
or hypocritical or insensitive adults, Harry's solitude and his
inability to escape his youthful memories are instead rooted
in the fact that the love and beauty that the Messingers
brought to his life have never been duplicated. His father's
bluffness and his mother's sharpness and their marital bick-
ering are no match for Herr Messinger's selfless love for his
wife, a love that inspired him to reclaim the overgrown land
at Cloverhill, or her desire to bring joy to others through
the imaginary worlds of movies.

Though Trevor infuses the Messingers with a fairytale
quality, he does not let us forget reality: the expatriated couple clings to love and beauty while their homelands are at war
with each other; the magic they bring to the all-too-real
world of provincial Ireland ultimately survives only in the
memory of the middle-aged proprietor of an empty cinema.
And as much as both the Messingers and Harry are sympathetically portrayed, the essential unreality of their daily lives
in Ireland reminds us of the impossibility of living outside history. The Messingers are "messengers" of hope and beauty,
but their relocation to a neutral island in the midst of catastrophe results in an unsustainable happiness. But though
Trevor has sometimes faulted his characters, particularly the
Anglo-Irish Big House denizens, for attempting to live ahis-
torically, the Messingers are treated compassionately. Unlike,

for instance, the Pulvertafts in "The News from Ireland", who disregard history because doing so helps them justify their position of privilege, the Messingers attempt to bring beauty and comfort to the country that has offered them sanctuary.

In recent years, provincial Ireland has felt the dramatic changes taking place throughout the country — the diminished power of the Catholic Church, the economic upswing nicknamed the "Celtic Tiger", the women's movement, the incursions of foreign cultures through the European Union and the steady influx of tourists and immigrants. Though Trevor is certainly cognisant of these changes, the characters in his fiction about provincial Ireland often remain unaffected by them. As Dolores MacKenna has observed, "This is the Ireland which Trevor left in 1954. In his work, the outward details may have altered but essentially things have remained the same" (1999, 158).

Though Trevor frequently visits Ireland, he has not lived there for nearly 50 years, and he is well aware that contemporary Ireland is not the place where he spent his early life.

> I think of someone like myself now as interminably beyond the pale, looking in, when I think of Ireland. I think I see Ireland more clearly through the wrong end of a telescope rather than the other way round. I listen to RTE and read *The Irish Times* every day of my life. It's easy to keep in touch, with the telephone and all the rest of it. However, not living in Ireland means that when I come here I'm struck by what a different place it is from when I was a child and a student. The 1950s, for instance, as a time of extraordinary tranquillity in Ireland. It's not a tranquil country now. At the same time, I always feel changes are superficial changes. They're surface changes. The Ireland that I think of with great affection is still there. (Ní Anluain, 2000: 224)

Perhaps in acknowledgement of the distance he feels, Trevor in recent years has often set his provincial fiction in the Ireland of the 1940s and 1950s, perhaps feeling that he can achieve greater verisimilitude in depicting the world with which he was once intimately acquainted. But these stories are hardly "period pieces", for their portrayal of dignity in the face of hardship, fantasy in response to stultifying reality, is timeless. Further, even when Trevor locates his provincial fiction in present time, his Ireland is not so static as it appears. Though still a place of limited opportunity — social, economic, and sexual — his contemporary Ireland is a place where religious institutions and social mores no longer exercise the unquestioned authority to stifle the individual. If some of Trevor's provincial Irish continue to live thwarted lives, they are now more likely to be immobilised by their own psyches. And in some stories — "Big Bucks" and "The Hill Bachelors" (see Chapter Eight), for instance — Trevor's characters are given a choice that their author did not have: remaining in the provincial Ireland that continues to compel their author's imagination.

Chapter Three

Writing the Troubles

In 1975, when "The Distant Past" appeared as part of the collection *Angels at the Ritz*, William Trevor had begun to carve a modest niche in Irish literary history. His student days in Dublin and the influence of James Joyce had inspired his only Irish novel to date, *Mrs Eckdorf in O'Neill's Hotel*; the stories of the limitations and frustrations of living in rural and provincial Ireland for which he has demonstrated a seemingly inexhaustible gift had begun to appear, including the still-beloved "The Ballroom of Romance".

But by the mid-1970s, it must have become apparent even to an expatriate Irishman of long standing that all was "changed, changed utterly" at home. British military occupation, the civil rights marches, Bloody Sunday, civil strife in Northern Ireland, and acts of terrorism were gripping international attention and transforming both Irish life and Irish literature. Undoubtedly, as the Northern conflict spilled into acts of violence in England itself, Trevor felt dismay and concern at the unfolding catastrophe; as an Irishman living in England, he certainly must have been aware of the increasing hostility and distrust with which the English viewed Irish expatriates. By the 1970s, Trevor's chronological distance from Ireland had widened, but his emotional engagement with it had begun to take a new direction. In a handful of short stories written in the 1970s and early 1980s, Trevor began to examine the contagion of violence and the longevity of history. Within a few years, Ireland's colonial struggle would become the predominant subject of some of his finest fiction.

In Trevor's early stories concerning Irish civil strife, characters discover that geographical, chronological, and emotional distance cannot protect their lives from being disrupted by violence. Present violence opens past wounds in "The Distant Past", but provokes an ultimately thwarted desire for reconciliation of old hostilities in "Attracta" and "Saints". In "Autumn Sunshine", "Beyond the Pale", and "Another Christmas", characters discover that they cannot insulate themselves against violence and suffering, however seemingly far removed it may be from their daily lives.

In "The Distant Past", Trevor shows how a community once torn by hatred has put aside bitterness and lived peacefully for years — only to disintegrate into distrust and hostility once again. The Middletons, elderly Anglo-Irish Protestants, are the last remnants of an Ascendancy family whose once-elegant Big House is now a decaying ruin. Although in the early years of Irish independence they accept local gossip and prejudicially blame their adversity on the alleged rapaciousness of their late father's Catholic mistress and on the changes brought by the new Irish state, they have learned to live amicably with the very Catholic neighbours who during the Irish Civil War had forcibly occupied their home in an attempt to ambush English soldiers.

Yet though the Middletons have weathered the past, they have not forgotten it. Despite Irish independence, the brother and sister have continued a stalwart allegiance to England:

> They rose to their feet when the BBC played "God Save the King", and on the day of the coronation of Queen Elizabeth II they drove into the town with a

> small Union Jack propped up in the back window of
> their Ford Anglia. (*CS*, 351)

Even in the present time of the story, the 1970s, the Middletons sit in their crumbling house and recall their father, who
had met Queen Victoria:

> even in their middle-sixties they could still hear him
> saying that God and Empire and Queen formed a
> trinity unique in any worthy soldier's heart. In the
> hall hung the family crest, and on ancient Irish linen
> the Cross of St George. (352)

As the Middletons become more elderly and impoverished,
Fat Driscoll/Cranley (Trevor altered the name for the 1992
Collected Stories), the very man who had once taken over
their home, jokes about the enmity of the past, and Miss
Middleton feels a kinship with him, as they are both childless
and both suffering the effects of ageing. In a delicate consideration of the Middletons' straitened finances, Cranley, now
the town butcher, assures them that the chopped meat he
provides free of charge for their Irish setter is of no use to
him. They look forward to their weekly visits to town, where
they sell eggs and enjoy drinks and conversation with their
Catholic neighbours. The Middletons are treated as a cherished anachronism, even as a tourist attraction, for the town
prospers into a thriving vacation spot whose visitors marvel
at the ability of former enemies to live together peacefully.

But as Trevor often shows us, history cannot be so easily ignored or escaped. When violence erupts in the North
in the 1960s, the townspeople attempt to convince themselves that it has nothing to do with them. In fact, their town
is but 60 miles from the border, and as violence spreads
beyond Belfast and Derry, the tourist trade evaporates, the
town's cherished prosperity eroded. The Middletons become the scapegoats for this reversal of fortune, and are

now snubbed by the very people who once treated them kindly, including Fat Cranley, who now regrets his former charity and wishes instead to be remembered for his militancy during the Civil War.

Ironically, the revival of old bitterness toward the Middletons is triggered not by concern about Northern civil rights but by a threatened economy. The fragile harmony that once existed between the Middletons and their Catholic neighbours is transformed into discordant notes from the past; the loyalty to England that once elicited the amusement of their neighbours now has ominous implications: "Had they driven with a Union Jack now they would, astoundingly, have been shot" (355). Their dog, one of the last remnants of the past, dies — a symbolic event, for he had been a key element in the tenuous link between the Middletons and their neighbours. They remove from their home all vestiges of their English heritage "in mourning for the *modus vivendi* that had existed so long between them and the people of the town" (355). They are left a pathetic old couple in a crumbling home, with nothing but death to look forward to: "Because of the distant past they would die friendless. It was worse than being murdered in their beds" (356).

Though the Middletons are pitiable, they also embody the flawed understanding so often pointed up in depictions of Ascendancy families and which would receive more sustained scrutiny in Trevor's "The News from Ireland". As Christensen and Pihl rightly observe, the Middletons evince "an almost total unawareness of Irish history and its reverberations in the present" (1989, 207), yet, ironically, live in a Big House with an Irish name, Carraveagh, and enjoy the companionship of an Irish setter named Turloch, "a traditional name of Irish chieftains" (211). Further, their attitude toward the changing state of Ireland bespeaks an arrogance based on privilege. Their initial reaction to Irish independence is that "The revolutionary regime would not last, they quietly informed the Reverend Packham: what sense was there in green-painted pillar-boxes and a language that no-body understood?" (*CS*, 349–50). When Fat Cranley describes the early incidents of violence in the North as "'a bad business'" and comments, "'We don't want that stuff all over again'", Miss Middleton replies, "'We didn't want it in the first place'" (353). Despite the fact that Cranley laughs along with the Middletons, the remark reveals a startling insensitivity as well as a profound ignorance of her own place in Irish history. But Miss Middleton simply cannot believe that public events impinge on private lives: "Yes, it was a game, she thought: how could any of it be as real or as important as the afflictions and problems of the old butcher himself, his rheumatism and his reluctance to retire?" (353).

Though it has been described as "perhaps the earliest of Trevor's Troubles stories" (Rhodes, 1983: 98), "The Distant Past" provides a glimpse of the growing complexity of Trevor's attitude toward Ireland. The desire for and failure of human relationships that Gregory Schirmer has identified as being central to Trevor's fiction is certainly present, as is "his continuing exploration of the ways in which apparently dead events of past conflicts obtrude on the present and shape the future" (Rhodes, 1983: 98–9). Yet "The Distant Past" also prefigures Trevor's later concern with Empire and its consequences: the evils wrought by the imbalance of and abuses of power, the far-reaching impact of ignorance. Nurtured as they are in the imperialist values of their late father, raised to think of themselves as superior, the Middletons, poor and elderly, are now rendered powerless. But the attitudes that shaped their family are implicitly dangerous, as Trevor will demonstrate in such later masterpieces as "The News from Ireland" and *The Silence in the Garden*.

In the 1978 collection, *Lovers of Their Time*, "Another Christmas" depicts how sectarian violence reaches far beyond Northern Ireland to undermine human relationships for an Irish Catholic family living in England. Norah and Dermot left Ireland 20 years previously because employment opportunities were more attractive in England, but as a result they have become strangers in a strange land. Norah, who had pressured her husband to emigrate, blames herself for the fact that her children have English accents and now view England as their home.

Norah and Dermot have adjusted to English life, but an outbreak of IRA bombings in England leads to the estrangement of the Irish couple from their one true English friend, Mr Joyce. (By naming this loyal Englishman after a writer so essentially identified with Ireland, Trevor makes it clear that easy categories simply will not do in this story.)

Joyce, their landlord, has over the years become a member of their family, but although all three deplore violence, Dermot once observes that "The bombs were a crime but it didn't do to forget that the crime would not be there if generations of Catholics in the North had not been treated as animals" (*CS*, 519). Norah intuitively knows that the remark will be offensive and hurries to condemn the violence; but the incident destroys a friendship.

Now, at Christmastime, she is convinced that Joyce will remain estranged from them forever unless her husband tries to make amends. His refusal to acknowledge that anything is wrong causes her to question her love for him.

> Everyone knew that the Catholics in the North had suffered, that generations of injustice had been twisted into the shape of a cause. But you couldn't say it to an old man who had hardly been outside Fulham in his life. You couldn't say it because when you did it sounded like an excuse for murder. (520)

Norah also realises that Irish violence in England has made her family's position precarious; she envisions a time when she and Dermot will be unwelcome in their chosen homeland.

She is also convinced that her husband's obstinacy has implicated them in violence: "She cleared up the tea-things, reflecting that the bombers would be pleased if they could note the victory they'd scored in a living-room in Fulham" (495).

"Another Christmas" ultimately poses no easy answers. In view of Dermot's rather mild expostulation, Schirmer's characterisation of him as defending "an intense commitment to political ideology" (1990, 140) is absurd, but at the same time, Dermot's resolute refusal to acknowledge the depth of Joyce's alienation is maddening, not only to his wife but to the reader as well. Although Norah's increasing sense of isolation is pitiable, her insularity is likewise unsettling, as when she declares, "'I never yet cared for a North of Ireland person, Catholic or Protestant. Let them fight it out and not bother us'" (520). We understand Norah's desire to preserve harmony in family and friendship alike; we also recognise that in the world of Trevor's fiction her disavowal of connection with other suffering people — and with Irish history — is both short-sighted and morally questionable. Finally, we pity the isolation of the elderly Joyce, but his own intransigence brings into question Norah's belief that their Irishness had made no difference to him. If Dermot's comment that injustice and violence are connected in Northern Ireland causes Joyce to turn his back on a decades-long friendship, perhaps the connection between the Irish expatriates and their English landlord was far more tenuous than either was willing to admit.

"Attracta", which began life as a BBC radio play and was later recast as a short story included in *Lovers of Their Time*, portrays a character whose life has been directly affected by Irish civil strife. Though one critic asserts that her "life has been all but ruined" (Core, 1993: 6), Attracta in fact has lived happily despite the catastrophe that orphaned her as a child. Attracta gradually discovers that her parents' deaths were caused by her kindly friends and surrogate parents, Mr

Devereux and his onetime lover, Geraldine Carey, in an abortive attempt to ambush English soldiers. The couple spends the rest of their lives attempting to atone through kindness to the orphaned child. Attracta discovers the truth through the venomous outbursts of rabid, Catholic-hating Mr Purce, but his attempts to fill her with hatred of people she has come to love are ineffectual.

Attracta's inner peace is shattered many years later when she reads a horrific news account of the rape and suicide of Penelope Vade, an Englishwoman whose soldier husband had been murdered in Northern Ireland, his decapitated head sent to her through the mail. Penelope's joining the Women's Peace Movement in Northern Ireland, "to make the point that somehow neither he nor she had been defeated" (CS, 676) apparently enraged her husband's killers, who gang-raped her and drove her to final despair.

Attracta is understandably horrified by this inhuman event, but she also discovers a kinship with this tragic young woman. Trevor's naming her for an early Irish saint is surely apt, for not only has she forgiven her parents' murderers, her intense feeling of identification with Penelope Vade is the essence of empathy. She relives the young woman's horror at the grisly discovery of her husband's severed head; she mentally drags herself across the floor with the despairing, dying Penelope. She undergoes what Michael Ponsford has called "the spasm of imagination so frequently felt by Trevor's characters when they are confronted by a truth" (1988: 84). As is so often the case with such characters, imaginativeness carries the price of social ostracism. Attracta and others like her (for instance, Cynthia Strafe from the later "Beyond the Pale") are thwarted artists whose vision is manifested in evocative but ultimately impotent speech: no one wants to hear the uncomfortable stories they bear.

Attracta experiences a life-altering revelation, yet discovers sadly that no one will share her enlightenment. She
tries to arouse in her young students her own awareness of
the senselessness of violence and the necessity of halting its
continuation; she tells them her own story and that of Penelope Vade. But these children are so inured to violence that
even Penelope's story fails to shock them. "'Sure, isn't there
stuff like that in the papers the whole time?' one of the children suggested" (687). For Attracta, her own life offers a
hope that Penelope never found: violent people *can* change.
She pleads with her students to share the lesson:

> "If only she had known," Attracta said, "that there
> was still a faith she might have had, that God does
> not forever withhold His mercy. Will those same
> men who enacted that vengeance on her one day
> keep bees and budgerigars? Will they serve in shops
> and be kind to the blind and the deaf? Will they gar-
> den in the evening and be good fathers? It is not im-
> possible." (688)

But Attracta's efforts are ultimately ineffectual. She is pressured into retirement because parents have been shocked
and angered that she would talk in the classroom about rape
and murder — the same violent crimes of which the children are all too aware. George Core's comment that because of Attracta's reflections about her own past and the
Vades' tragedy she "gradually but inexorably runs off the
rails" (1993, 6) misses Trevor's emphatic point that it is the
world, not Attracta, that has gone mad.

"Attracta" is one of Trevor's darkest stories, for the
only person who seems to want to put an end to atrocity is
ultimately silenced. And, by giving Attracta a saint's name
and investing her with a saint's charity, Trevor underlines
the near-impossibility that her message will be heard. And
though the story is perhaps Trevor's most gripping and

graphic treatment of the Troubles, it is not his most complex treatment of the issue, for we are not encouraged to
feel any ambivalence toward the characters. Purce's vicious
bigotry is deplorable; Devereux's and Carey's repentance is
commendable; Attracta's charity is admirable; violence is
evil. In "Attracta", we are not encouraged to take political
sides — and as Morrison has pointed out,

> . . . by not identifying the murderers in any way
> (though readers familiar with the actual situation in
> Belfast will assume they were Provos or some other
> nominally Catholic anti-British group), Trevor down-
> plays the neat categorisations and oversimplifications
> that are the stuff of bigotry and focuses instead on
> the horror and gratuitousness of the acts of violence
> themselves. (1993, 86)

The didacticism and graphic descriptions of violence in the
story, both uncharacteristic of Trevor, may be rooted in the
story's origins as a radio play, a medium that requires vivid
description and direct presentation of ideas. But it also
seems likely that Trevor was attempting to shock his audience, as Attracta attempts to jolt her students out of an indifference wrought by daily exposure to violence.

In 1981, "Saints", a precursor to the later novel *Fools of
Fortune*, appeared in *Atlantic Monthly*. Because of the two
works' close connection, the story will be discussed at
length in a later chapter. However, it should be mentioned
here that "Saints" in some respects plays a variation on the
themes of "Attracta". Like Attracta, the Anglo-Irish narrator
has suffered a brutal act of violence against his family; unlike
Attracta's, his life has been blighted by the experience, as is
manifested in his sensuality, heavy drinking, and inability to
form close relationships with people. But summoned back to
Ireland by a dying former family servant, the only other survivor of the attack on his family, the narrator experiences

what he sees as a "miracle": the pious Josephine enables him to release long-pent-up emotions, to recover some of his lost humanity. Rhodes sees an ironic link between "Saints" and "Attracta":

> . . . because she has never forgotten the past, Josephine brings it into the present and is able to console an old man; whereas, ironically, Attracta, who was able to forget the past because of the goodness of others, cannot bring the lessons of the past into the present for anyone but herself. (1983, 108)

Two stories in the 1981 collection *Beyond the Pale* probe more deeply into history's repetitions by scrutinising the very nature of colonisation.

Like Attracta, Canon Moran of "Autumn Sunshine" finds past and present Irish political turmoil impinging upon his quiet, essentially happy life. But, unlike Attracta, he ultimately chooses not to be disturbed by the implications of that intrusion.

In this autumnal story, the beauty of the season is interwoven, as in Keats's ode, with its natural melancholy. The golden hues of the landscape are also harbingers of the death of the year, and this tension is reflected in Moran's own life. Autumn was Mrs Moran's favourite season, but Frances Moran is dead, and her husband grieves for a wife he continues to love devotedly.

Regretting the loss of the beloved wife who has maintained harmony both within the parish and with their Catholic neighbours, Canon Moran is surprised and pleased by a visit from his long-estranged daughter, Deirdre. But his pleasure is clouded by the presence of Deirdre's shadowy boyfriend, Harold, an Englishman whose passion for Irish history is matched by his bitterness toward his native country. Canon Moran distrusts Harold's interest in his daughter and in Ireland itself, believing that both are simply a means of venting his hatred against England:

> Harold was an Englishman who had espoused a cause because it was one through which the status quo of his own country might be damaged. Similar such Englishmen, read about in newspapers, stirred in the clergyman's mind: men from Ealing and Liverpool and Wolverhampton who had changed their names to Irish names, who had even learned the Irish language, in order to ingratiate themselves with the new Irish revolutionaries. Such men dealt out death and chaos, announcing that their conscience insisted on it. (*CS*, 847)

Canon Moran lives in Wexford, the county most closely identified with the 1798 rebellion, and Harold becomes avidly interested in Kinsella's Barn, scene of the brutal murder by one Sergeant James of twelve men and women suspected of sheltering enemies of England during the rebellion. Following the murders, Kinsella, an innocent man, was himself murdered in retribution for the deaths that took place on his property.

But whereas Harold leaps upon the massacre at Kinsella's Barn as a symbol of Ireland's continuing oppression, Canon Moran finds in the incident another lesson. Like many of the Anglo-Irish in Trevor's fiction, Moran is removed from and largely unaware of Irish history: "He began to say that Irish history had always been of considerable interest to him, also that it had a good story to it, its tragedy uncomplicated" (843). This appalling ignorance is rattled by his conversations with Harold, and this new enlightenment convinces Moran of the evil of perpetuating violence. Just as Attracta had tried unsuccessfully to reach her students, Canon Moran preaches to his bewildered parishioners about Kinsella's Barn, the futility of violence, and the necessity for forgiveness. Just as Harold has connected Ireland's contemporary political struggle with 1798, Canon Moran privately links Sergeant James and Harold, wondering whether James, like Harold with his facial birthmark, was somehow disfigured or disabled and found in violence a private vengeance against an unfair world.

Yet for Canon Moran the lesson is incomplete:

> Canon Moran's one moment of insight does not seem to include forgiveness of the people who murdered Kinsella. Here as elsewhere there is no doubt as to the sincerity of the Canon's feelings; but preaching forgiveness for atrocities committed by an English sergeant in 1798 may not, in the nature of things, seem unnatural to an Anglo-Irish Protestant clergyman whose naïve sense of Irish history is one aspect of his self-deception. (Christensen and Pihl, 1989: 214)

In fact, the story does not indicate that in his sermon Moran singles out Sergeant James for forgiveness. The only part of the sermon that is quoted in the story is Moran's condemnation of *Kinsella's* murder, and his primary lesson seems to be that vengeance is both evil and futile. But Christensen and Pihl are surely correct in their contention that Moran has not learned his lesson fully, for Moran's ignorance of history renders him unable to fathom the injustice and bitterness that continue to manifest themselves in violence. His message of forgiveness, though pious, is naïve. Further, though both Sergeant James and Kinsella occupy his thoughts, there is no indication that he is particularly troubled by the gruesome deaths of the original victims at Kinsella's Barn.

Though he suspects that Harold and Deirdre may be planning terrorist activities, he also acknowledges his own frailty of being jealous of all the men who have courted his daughters, and he dismisses his suspicions as mere paternal jealousy. The Canon's first impression may be correct, for circumstantial evidence throughout the story suggests that Harold and Deirdre are contemplating violence. But Moran finds it more comfortable to imagine how his dead wife would allay his fears, and he conjures up her soothing image.

> . . . Moran's change is only to put the past firmly into the past once again and to determine not to accept and deal with the reality he had earlier perceived: that Harold is really a contemporary Sergeant James. When he calls up Frances it is for her to do what she has always done — resolve his problem for him, here by denying that Harold is like James. (Rhodes, 1983: 109)

The story is actually far more ambiguous than the above passage suggests. Harold may well be a dangerous man — or he may be, as Moran would like to believe, all talk.

"Autumn Sunshine" is a far more complex story than it first appears. It may be read as another instance of Trevor's pointing up the terrible longevity of violence, the painful tendency of family members to become alienated, the sad failure of communication. But the story also examines the very process of colonisation, for Harold, the disaffected Englishman, is practising a new imperialism.

Privately bemoaning his daughter's attachment to a man he cannot like, Moran suspects that Harold's interest in Deirdre has a sinister dimension:

> She was like a zombie, her father thought. She was being used because she was an Irish girl; she was Harold's Irish connection, and in some almost frightening way she believed herself in love with him. (847)

Christensen and Pihl have noted the Anglicisms in Deirdre's speech, affectations that make her sound insincere and underline her "zombie-like dependence on Harold" (1989,

213). Deirdre may in fact be part of Harold's "radical chic"; her nationality gives her a particular cachet. And though it is certainly possible that what Harold and Deirdre share is "rebellion against their backgrounds and established society" (1989, 213), it is disturbing that Deirdre, who once had the gumption to rebel against her parents and leave home, is now apparently will-less in Harold's presence.

Further, as several critics have noted, Deirdre's name is itself symbolically loaded, connecting her with the tragic heroine of Irish myth. As will be discussed in a later chapter, the mythical Deirdre is often identified with Ireland itself, the country portrayed in literature and political cartoons as a sorrowful woman. Trevor, who consistently resists such female iconography in his fiction, does so as well in "Autumn Sunshine". Harold's attempts to, in effect, colonise Deirdre are portrayed in a dim light.

Trevor's "Autumn Sunshine" is a study of colonisation, an early manifestation of an insistent preoccupation in Trevor's later Irish fiction. Deirdre, whose Anglo-Irish upbringing leaves her ignorant of her own country's history, adopts the version of history espoused by her English lover — a story of Ireland as victim. Her echoing of his linguistic patterns recalls the erosion of Ireland's own language in the face of English occupation. Whether or not Harold will act on his violent feelings against England, his violence against Deirdre's sense of self is very real indeed. If he in fact enlists Deirdre in political terrorism, his actions will likely have little to do with Ireland's independence, but will more probably be an act of private vengeance.

In "Beyond the Pale", Trevor examines Irish colonialism in an allegorical reading of Ireland's political turmoil. The four English tourists who annually visit Glencorn Lodge, a hotel on the Antrim coast, are to varying degrees colonists engaged in the process that Declan Kiberd has named "inventing Ireland". The English tourists' Ireland is thoroughly

sanitised and Anglicised. The hotel's English proprietors, tellingly named Malseed (and Mrs Malseed was formerly Miss
Saxton), have reclaimed a derelict estate and transformed it
into a carefully controlled environment — a hotel that does
not advertise but whose proprietors rely on the verbal rec-
ommendations of the "right sort of people". With its pre-
ciously named rooms (Rose, Geranium, Fuchsia, etc.) and its
pervasive decorum and avoidance of anything deemed unpleasant, Glencorn Lodge is an unreal, elitist world.

Only one of the four tourists, Cynthia Strafe, whose surname is suggestively violent, takes any real interest in the
country she has visited for fourteen years. Her companions
— her husband, his longstanding mistress, Milly, and his
boarding-school chum, Dekko Deakin, view Ireland as a
pleasant site for bridge games, tweed-buying and sightseeing.
The Irish themselves are at best amusing, as embodied in the
friendly waitress, Kitty, and at worst profoundly disruptive —
the tortured young man whose tragic story and ultimate
death temporarily shake their complacency. Otherwise,
Strafe thinks nothing of telling an Irish joke; Milly character-
ises the local police as possessing a "natural slowness of intel-
lect" (*CS*, 758); Ireland's terrible civil strife is pondered only
to the extent that it might interfere with their holiday plans.
Only Cynthia chooses to immerse herself in Irish history and
geography, but her attempts to educate her companions are
either ignored or patronisingly tolerated.

Milly is an unreliable first-person narrator: shallow, self-
centred, waspish, and self-deluding, she likes Glencorn because there she carries on an adulterous affair with Strafe.
Milly frequently uses euphemism to romanticise her own
situation and to avoid confronting the realities of Ireland.
Through this process, Strafe is transformed from a cruel,
self-involved man into a long-suffering husband too noble
to leave his wife. Northern Ireland's civil strife is similarly

rendered into an "unpleasantness" that thankfully does not affect English people's holidays at Glencorn Lodge.

Milly's self-damaging narrative encourages the reader to sympathise with and trust Cynthia. In public, Milly treats Cynthia as an old friend, but her narrative is peppered with disparaging comments about her appearance, her domestic skills, and the fact that she "reads too much" (755)! Increasingly, it becomes apparent that if Milly dislikes Cynthia, then Cynthia must be worth the reader's attention.

Cynthia's complacency — or at least resignation — is rocked by her encounter with the troubled young Irishman, who earlier had been noted by her companions as being "not at all the kind of person one usually sees at Glencorn Lodge" (752). Despite Milly's comments on the man's "unkempt" appearance, his real objectionableness seems to be the fact that he is *Irish*, the only Irish guest in this English-dominated hotel. Because we receive the story of Cynthia's encounter twice-removed, as it were — Milly reports Cynthia's account of the man's story — it is impossible to know exactly how much he told Cynthia directly, how much her own imaginative empathy has contributed to the sad tale she shares with her indifferent companions, a story of a young man who murders his childhood sweetheart to halt her political violence: she has become a clandestine bomb-maker in England. Tormented by this act, he returns to Glencorn Lodge, whose grounds, before the arrival of the Malseeds, were once the scene of his romantic idyll.

Cynthia, distraught yet determined, tries in vain to persuade her companions that this couple's tragedy is part of a historical continuum in which the English are deeply implicated:

> "Just so much history it sounds like now, yet people starved or died while other people watched. A language was lost, a faith forbidden. Famine followed

revolt, plantation followed that. But it was people
who were struck into the soil of other people's land,
not forests of new trees; and it was greed and treachery that spread as a disease among them all. No wonder unease clings to these shreds of history and shots
ring out in answer to the mockery of drums. No
wonder the air is nervy with suspicion." (763)

The scene is unsettling both to Cynthia's audience and
Trevor's, for her speech becomes incantatory, even vatic, as
she "chanted in a singsong way that sounded thoroughly peculiar" the events that indicate to her the "chaos and contradiction" of Irish history. In fact, the chaos seems to have
touched Cynthia personally, as she scrambles that history's
chronology.

Yet she also recognises her and her companions' own
complicity in this history, for she recalls that when in the
past their placid domestic routine in England was inter-
rupted by news of atrocities in Northern Ireland, their predominant concern was that Glencorn Lodge and their
pleasant trips there should not be affected. Yet during this
arresting narrative, her companions are largely indifferent:
Milly thinks how unattractive Cynthia looks with her un-
combed hair and rumpled dress, and hopes that the incident
will not spoil their entire visit. Dekko makes ineffectual
clucks of sympathy to calm Cynthia's outburst; her husband
is embarrassed and eventually angry that she is making a
public scene. Mr Malseed first attempts to placate Cynthia
and detach himself from the "unpleasantness" in the North:
"'There is unrest here, Mrs Strafe, but we do our best to
live with it'" (767). Only when Cynthia's increasingly passionate speech draws the attention of the other guests does
Malseed's calm veneer begin to crack, and he angrily asserts,
"'You are trying to bring something to our doorstep which
most certainly does not belong here'" (768), a symbolic

statement, for not only does Malseed refuse to be involved with the Irish couple's deaths, he speaks in the proprietary voice of a true imperialist: Ireland is a possession and would be a perfect place if only the Irish would go away.

Recognising her own complicity in colonialism, Cynthia confesses to Kitty, the Irishwoman who has served the English tourists on all their visits:

> "Through honey-tinted glasses we love you and we love your island, Kitty. We love the lilt of your racy history, we love your earls and heroes. Yet we made a sensible pale here once, as civilised people create a garden, pretty as a picture." (769)

She now understands that such a romanticisation of Ireland has a grim underside. She cannot dismiss the Irish couple's deaths as isolated incidents, for "'evil breeds evil in a mysterious way'" (769): their tragedy belongs to Irish history as much as the Act of Union, the Statutes of Kilkenny, and the other notable events she attempts to explain to her bored companions.

Only when the confession takes a more personal turn, and Cynthia admits her knowledge of Strafe's affair with the "vicious" Milly, his own unspecified but "perverted" sexual proclivities, the unspecified schoolboy trauma that has blighted Dekko's life despite his and Strafe's crushingly boring nostalgia about those years, does she finally hit a nerve with her companions. Yet there is no indication that her speech has worked any enlightenment: her three companions are seemingly affected only by her pointed personal remarks. Milly experiences only a partial revelation, realising that Strafe will never leave Cynthia but deluding herself that it is because he is "honourable in his own particular way" (771), not the more likely explanation that he is selfishly unwilling to disrupt his comfortable life for a woman who makes no demands upon him and complaisantly indulges his taste for sexual practices that disgust his wife. Dekko's normally breezy manner is profoundly shaken, but evidently more by Cynthia's revelations about his private life than by the sufferings of the Irish. Strafe, who wanted so urgently to avoid a scene, causes the most embarrassment by shouting at Cynthia that she is a "'fleshless ugly bitch'" (770).

Like Attracta and so many of Trevor's other characters who voice unpleasant truths in the hopes of effecting change, Cynthia's message does not seem to make the desired impact, though she voices the hope that perhaps truth can catalyse a new beginning. Yet that hope is overshadowed by Milly's final words. With unselfconscious irony she complains of a pain "where perhaps my heart is" (771), and wishes that Cynthia could have drowned as the young Irishman had. Cynthia's words linger in the air, but their effect seems negligible:

> Her awful rigmarole hung about us as the last of the
> tea things were gathered up — the earls who'd fled,
> the famine and the people planted. The children were
> there too, grown up into murdering riff-raff. (771)

Scrambling the chronology of Irish history (as Cynthia does, but with a difference) and evincing little comprehension of it, learning no sympathy for the blighted lives of the young couple, Milly can think only of her own frustrations.

"Beyond the Pale" moves Trevor in a new direction. As with previous stories, it underlines the evils wrought by abuses of power both in personal relationships and historical moments; it emphasises the responsibility of the individual to be aware of the "world beyond that of the self" (Schirmer, 1990: 144); it stresses the futility and contagion of violence. But "Beyond the Pale" is also a symbolic rendering of Irish history and Anglo-Irish relations. The English tourists manifest attitudes representative of England's toward Ireland throughout history — idealisation, hostility, proprietorship, paternalism, ignorance. Glencorn Lodge is a colony in miniature, a

Pale, a little England on the island of Ireland yet where the Irish are unwelcome visitors. The sad, futile story of the young couple is itself a microcosm of Irish history. The young woman embraces violence in response to political inequity; the young man abhors violence, yet commits it to prevent further violence, then turns violently against himself. The Irish couple dies; the English return home relatively unscathed.

The two Englishwomen, Cynthia and Milly, themselves evince colonial responses to Ireland, though only Cynthia eventually recognises her error. In the past, she has loved Ireland's beauty and apparent tranquillity, but her eager reading on Irish subjects, including the very historical events she recites in her moment of truth, has rendered her merely a useful "guide book". There is no indication that prior to her encounter with the young man she was particularly upset or guilt-ridden about her own country's part in Ireland's suffering. Yet eventually Cynthia discovers in Ireland the heart of her own darkness, for there she acknowledges her own guilt in being a passive observer not only of her husband's infidelity and Milly's treachery, but of the years of inequity and injustice that lie beneath the pleasant, unreal patina of Glencorn Lodge. In a pattern frequently found in English colonial literature, Cynthia leaves the familiarity of her own country and discovers through the "other" the dimensions of herself kept firmly in check when she is at home.

As we have seen, Milly's self-absorption and sense of superiority to the Irish render her impervious to her surroundings except to the extent that they enhance or impinge upon her personal comfort. Yet Milly's behaviour also recalls Declan Kiberd's observation that English prejudice toward and stereotyping of the Irish frequently involved ascribing to the Irish the very qualities the English disliked or sought to avoid in themselves (1995, 30). Milly speaks of the Irish youth as "murdering riff-raff" just at the moment when she herself is wishing Cynthia dead. Further, despite the carefully courteous, rigidly controlled demeanours manifested by the English characters in the story, we are well aware that strong passions — sex, anger, and violence — roil beneath the surface, as Dekko's tearfulness, Strafe's venom, and Malseed's anger reveal.

The title is another indication of the story's larger symbolic implications. "Beyond the Pale" has, of course, multiple meanings, and Kristin Morrison has noted the varied uses of the word "pale" in the story (1993, 91) The Pale has a specific historical meaning: a palpable structure erected by the English in the fourteenth century to separate colonised and therefore "civilised" Ireland from the untamed country beyond. "Beyond the pale" has increasingly taken on a more generic meaning, however: to be "beyond the pale" is to be not quite right, unacceptable, outside the range of proper society, etc. Trevor plays on numerous readings of the expression: Glencorn Lodge is itself a type of pale, and the English visitors have deliberately isolated themselves from the political struggle raging around them; the Irishman who triggers Cynthia's epiphanic moment is himself "beyond the pale", for his clothes, his red hair, his apparent Irishness render him unwelcome at Glencorn. Only when the world beyond the pale of the quiet hotel intrudes itself in the form of the man's suicide must that world be dealt with by the self-satisfied English.

Finally, "beyond the pale" is part of the story's essential message. Cynthia has peered over the pale and discovered devastating truths about herself and her country. When, at the end of the story, she expresses the tentative wish that her words can effect some change in her and her companions' lives, Trevor also seems to be providing an early glimpse of his own vision of Anglo-Irish relations. As long as a mentality of "Pale" and "Beyond the Pale" exists, with its attendant abuses of power, harmful stereotyping, and mutual distrust, Irish history will continue to repeat itself. In his introductory comments in *The Field Day Anthology of Irish Writing*, John Wilson Foster noted of "Beyond the Pale":

> [Not only Cynthia's saga but the entire action of the story is perhaps an allegory of the original English colony in Ireland (the Pale), British hypocrisy about and ignorance of Ireland from then until the present, and the likelihood of British withdrawal after a crisis and a British awakening to the reality of the island.] (1991, 1007)

Foster's comment is at once too tentative ("perhaps an allegory") and too optimistic a reading of Trevor's story, for by the end only Cynthia shows signs of "British awakening", and she is viewed by her companions as irrational and annoying.

In these early stories of the Troubles, Trevor turns over the rock of Anglo-Irish history and scrutinises the repugnant creatures concealed beneath: bigotry, sadism, and violence. Yet although Trevor's Troubles fiction asserts that violence is a futile and soul-deadening enterprise, he also meticulously avoids easy categories that reduce people to expected roles or labels and ignore their complex albeit thorny humanity.

Chapter Four

A "Lace Curtain" Protestant in the Big House

William Trevor has described himself as a "small-town Irish Protestant", a "'lace-curtain' Protestant" (Stout, 1989–90: 131). He distinguishes himself from the Protestant landed gentry that came to be known in the eighteenth century as the Ascendancy, a class that evolved from centuries of land usurpation and religious discrimination and whose estate houses separating them from the displaced Irish assumed the peculiar designation of the "Big House":

> The Big House was most often constructed of native limestone in alien architectural forms by the represen-tatives of a colonial power. It was built on land usually expropriated by men and women who considered themselves Irish, but who were caught between two countries and two identities, separated from their tenants not only by class but by religion, language, and national origin as well. (Kreilkamp, 1998: 7)

Throughout the nineteenth and early twentieth centuries, the Big House culture began to erode due to economic and political changes. The declining power of the Anglo-Irish and the emergence of an independent, Catholic-dominated state was reflected in the fates of the buildings themselves: many were destroyed in the Civil War of the 1920s or in later decades; others decayed because of their owners' straitened finances or took on new lives as museums, hotels, etc.

For over two centuries, the Big House has also lent its name to a literary tradition. Poets, playwrights, and novelists as diverse as Maria Edgeworth, Brendan Behan, Somerville and Ross, Lennox Robinson, Elizabeth Bowen and W.B. Yeats adopted varying attitudes toward the decay of the Big House: it was the doleful decline of a stately social order; the welcome demise of an oppressive tradition. The Big House and its attendant culture continue to compel such contemporary Irish writers as Aidan Higgins, John Banville, Molly Keane, Jennifer Johnston, and Trevor himself.

The Big House's continuing popularity as a motif in Irish fiction has drawn mixed reactions from Irish critics. Seamus Deane has expressed impatience with the Big House novel's longevity, viewing it not only as an exhausted vein but also as a continuation of detrimental myths about Ireland:

> The re-emergence of the Big House novel, with all its implicit assumptions, demonstrates the comparative poverty of the Irish novelistic tradition and the power of Yeats's presence even now. . . . It is surely time to abandon such a myth and find intellectual allegiance elsewhere. (1977, 321–2)

Andrew Parkin disagrees with such an assessment, noting that the disintegration of the Big House culture has provided "a powerful literary theme with rich implications" that "enables Irish novelists to deal with Ireland without confining themselves to it" (1988, 327):

> As Seamus Deane points out, as the Big House culture died it was resuscitated in Irish writing. Deane sees this as an "artificial" process. It is, on the

> contrary, entirely natural: the corpse is exhumed by
> some for the purposes of revenge; by others it is
> resurrected in the nostalgic and ambivalent imagina-
> tion, for they are its apologists and its critics. (309)

Like other chroniclers of the Big House, Trevor portrays a
disintegrating way of life. In several of these works — "The
Distant Past", *Fools of Fortune*, *The Silence in the Garden*,
"Saints" and *The Story of Lucy Gault* — past and present are
connected either evidently or implicitly. As readers, we par-
take of "then" and "now": prosperity and dissolution, the
old Ascendancy giving way to the new order. "The News
from Ireland", set in the Famine years, nevertheless pulls us
into the present: we feel the reverberations of the bigotry
and thoughtlessness that divide people, not only in present-
day Ireland, but throughout the world. Both *The Silence in
the Garden* and *The Story of Lucy Gault* employ the decline of a
Big House in allegorical readings of Irish history.

In Trevor's Big House fiction, the Ascendancy is neither
glorified nor condemned; there is neither an insider's regret-
ful nostalgia for former luxury nor the dispossessed Irish
person's triumphant scorn at the decline of a usurping class.
Recognising, as have other contemporary Big House writers,
that the fading of the Ascendancy "reaches deeply into human nature itself" (Kreilkamp, 1998: 327), Trevor has used
Big House settings to explore the theme of human alienation
and miscommunication, as he does in the short stories "The
Distant Past", "Saints" and "Timothy's Birthday" and in the
novel *Fools of Fortune*. Yet whereas this theme informs "The
News from Ireland", *The Silence in the Garden* and *The Story
of Lucy Gault*, it is also apparent that the Big House provides
Trevor with a powerful symbol in the construction of his
increasingly allegorical treatment of Irish history.

"The Distant Past", discussed in Chapter Three, prefigures Trevor's later treatments of the Big House, for it is a

melancholic statement on people's skills in misunderstanding and wounding each other. At the same time, the Middletons' insularity, ignorance of Irish history, and comprehension too late that they have failed to adjust to a changing Ireland renders them recognisable characters in the Big House tradition. Their Catholic neighbours' detachment from Northern Irish suffering until it affects them economically bespeaks Trevor's characteristic refusal to oversimplify the Irish.

Since the publication of "The Distant Past", the Big House has continued to interest Trevor. His first full-length stage play, *Scenes from an Album*, performed at the Abbey Theatre in 1981, dramatises episodes in the life of the Malcolmson family, from their 1610 acquisition of an estate in County Tyrone to their present-day decline. This brief play encapsulates Trevor's complex reading of the Big House as he explores it in subsequent fiction: the Malcolmsons are essentially decent people, but their very presence in Ireland has catastrophic consequences for themselves and those they have displaced, from the eviction of seventeenth-century tenants to the murder of a twentieth-century Malcolmson heir by Orangemen angry at his employment of Catholics on the family estate. The intervening years are riddled with other horrors: the arson killing of the gardener's elderly parents because of his engagement to a Protestant woman; his consequent mental breakdown and murder of his Malcolmson employer. The cycle of revenge and retribution deplored by Trevor throughout his Troubles fiction is very much in evidence here, its futility emphasised by the fact that the killers of Rafferty's parents are never identified, but because his sanity has been unhinged by the atrocity, he kills his employer because, as Annie Malcolmson asserts, "'he estimated that our kind were responsible for everything'" (*SA*, 24).

Anna and Honoria, fey twin daughters of the murdered man, visit their father's killer in the asylum, hoping to set an

example for their Protestant neighbours about forgiveness
and harmony. (In the later *The Story of Lucy Gault*, Lucy engages in a similar act of reconciliation, visiting Horahan, the
man who was the catalyst for her family's misery, and the
gesture by this Ascendancy woman moves her Catholic
neighbours.) Vowing to remain unmarried, they urge their
brother to follow their example and remain childless, to surrender the estate either to the descendant of the man dispossessed centuries earlier or to Catholic nuns. Though
their brother, Eustace (given name of all the Malcolmson
males), will not acquiesce to such a radical step, he does attempt to bring reconciliation to the community by employing both Protestants and Catholics, a step that results in his
murder by Orangemen and his sisters' disillusionment with
their formerly conciliatory attitude. At the play's end, the
murdered man's surviving son, now middle-aged, alcoholic,
and mentally ill, dreams of a different Ireland, crying, "Oh
God, tomorrow let the monster we brought with us be
gone" (*SA*, 40), but the scene ends with deafening sounds of
Orange marching, violence, and weeping. Demonising no
one, Trevor both acknowledges that the past cannot be un-
done and mourns its terrible repetitions.

Two subsequent novels, *Fools of Fortune* and *The Silence
in the Garden*, juxtapose past and present in delineating the
decline of two Ascendancy families. In the uncollected short
story "Saints" (1981), Trevor introduced some of the characters who were later to be the focus of *Fools of Fortune*
(1983). Both the story and the novel are concerned with the
aftermath of a brutal act of violence committed against an
Anglo-Irish family in 1918.

In "Saints", an elderly Irishman living in Italy is summoned home to the deathbed of Josephine, a former servant
to his family. He does not immediately reveal the reason for
his exile, and as Rhodes has noted, he is not at first a terribly
sympathetic character: ". . . we can easily conjure up a cross

between an old-time absentee landlord and a Roman sybarite, more a figure for contempt than compassion" (1983, 101). Clearly accustomed to privilege, the narrator without apparent regret recalls the rigours of Josephine's life as a family servant, and sees wry humour in his being asked to use mouthwash to mask his alcohol breath so as not to upset a woman whom he considers to be his social inferior.

The narrator gradually reveals that his distaste for Ireland stems from a ghastly family tragedy: the family estate, Kilneagh, was burned during the Troubles, resulting in the deaths of his father, two sisters, and the housekeeper. The gardener and his son, who attempted to help the family, were shot by the arsonists. The narrator's mother, unable to bear the suffering wrought by these atrocities, later kills herself. The narrator's emotional scars are less apparent, but nevertheless real. Not until the narrator confronts the dying Josephine can he regain the humanity so violently wrested from him.

Josephine, whose life has also been scarred by violence, has been living in a mental institution, where she is revered as a saint. As Sister Power tells him, Josephine has been credited with healing the sick; she prays for healing for those tortured by violence.

By some inexplicable means, Josephine has discovered the narrator's whereabouts in Italy, and by summoning him back to Ireland she forces him to confront his past and the truth about his own sad life. After Josephine's funeral he returns to his childhood home and relives the horror he has blocked out for so many years. Though after the experience he dulls his pain with his frequent escape, alcohol, he discovers what Josephine perhaps meant him to remember.

> I went away myself, hating the place, as I had on the day Josephine had brought me back there. But I remember her as she had been that day, how she had so very much wanted to make the journey, how she'd

> surprised me by kneeling in the yard and giving thanks
> for her life and for my mother's and for mine. (35)

When the narrator returns to Italy, Josephine's healing power goes with him. Muddled by wine, he recalls old legends of the saints, and as he drops off to sleep he realises that his saint, Josephine, has performed a miracle of her own. Her life has been one of self-sacrifice, of healing, of forgiveness, and now he recognises her final curing gesture. Josephine has given the narrator the gift of feeling emotion once again, an ability that had seemingly calcified in him.

When Trevor expanded and revised "Saints" into the novel *Fools of Fortune*, he made some notable changes. Whereas the unnamed narrator in "Saints" is compelled by financial concerns to return to Ireland yet chooses not to live there because his memories have caused him to dislike his homeland, Willie Quinton cannot live in Ireland because he has avenged his family's murder by killing the English soldier who supervised the atrocities. Unlike the short story's narrator, who has become bitter, possibly alcoholic, and sexually promiscuous, the exiled Willie continues to love his English cousin, Marianne, who unbeknownst to him became pregnant after their sole sexual encounter. Furthermore, Willie remembers Ireland with great tenderness, recalling his life before the tragedies with nostalgia and affection. Trevor implies that Willie's terrible act of vengeance is an anomaly:

> . . . a child can go through . . . what Willie went through and can be perfectly normal. But in the case of Willie — the whole point of the novel *Fools of Fortune* — is that there is a moment when you push the thing too far, and chance is too hard on you. Willie walked into the room and found his mother dead, that was too much. After his mother takes her life, his need for vengeance must have become impossible to ignore. After that, he just couldn't *live* a normal life

> . . . and it seems to me to be understandable that he
> couldn't — there's a sort of guilt and a dreadful
> shame that he would have felt. (Aronson, 1987: 8)

Rather than being told solely from Willie's point of view, *Fools of Fortune* blends Willie's narrative with the viewpoints of Marianne, his English cousin and lover, and Imelda, their child. This multiple narrative underlines the separations and misunderstandings that bedevil this sad family. Locked in their self-contained realities, whether by shortsightedness, prejudice, or, in Imelda's case, madness, this tragic trio embodies the terrible wastefulness of violence and revenge.

In *Fools of Fortune*, Trevor overturns expectations of the Big House. The child Willie Quinton, unlike George Arthur Pulvertaft in "The News from Ireland", is taught by an Irish Catholic priest, not an English Protestant governess, and he learns Irish history. His tutor, the pacifist Fr Kilgarriff, teaches Willie of his own admiration for Daniel O'Connell, the nineteenth-century political leader who successfully led the campaign known as Catholic Emancipation, which sought to end political discrimination against Catholics.

The Quintons themselves are an atypical Anglo-Irish family, living on a greatly diminished estate because their Famine-era ancestor returned the land to the dispossessed Irish. Pro-independence, they welcome Michael Collins to their home and provide him with financial support. Their household includes the defrocked Fr Kilgarriff and the elderly maid Philomena, left homeless by the death of the priest for whom she worked. The newly arrived maid, Josephine, discovers that she will not have to make special dietary arrangements on Fridays, for the Quintons, in deference to their Catholic servants, refrain from eating meat.

The Quintons' ghastly fate is likewise unconventional, for the violent deaths of Mr Quinton, his daughters, Deirdre and Geraldine, and the family servants Mrs Flynn, O'Neill, and his son, Tim Paddy, are perpetrated not by Irish Republicans but by the British-backed Black and Tans, who burn Kilneagh and shoot the witnesses. And although the heartbroken Mrs Quinton asserts that there is no connection, one cannot help but wonder how much the Quintons' pronationalist stance determined their fates.

In ascribing blame for the Quintons' murders, Trevor continues to undermine expectations, just as he has in his characterisation of this unconventional Big House family. In the novel's precursor, "Saints", the political affiliation of the killers was never specified, yet, ironically, two critics assume that Republicans are responsible: Rhodes asserts that the narrator's family was murdered by "die-hard republicans" (1983, 101); Kreilkamp argues that "the attackers on Kilneagh, because they remain unnamed, are presumably members of the IRA, who were ordinarily the perpetrators of violence against the Big House in the revolutionary period. . ." (1998, 223). Yet surely Trevor's ambiguity is deliberate here, intended to force the reader to abandon easy categorisation.

Trevor likewise undermines a common English stereotype of the Irish, a proclivity for violence, by making the characters most obsessed with violence not Irish, but English: the brutal Sergeant Rudkin oversees the murders at Kilneagh; English-born Evie Quinton, obsessed with revenge against Rudkin, precipitates terrible violence in her otherwise gentle son, who savagely murders Rudkin, stabbing him repeatedly and nearly decapitating him. In life, Evie was an even more ardent supporter of Irish independence than her Irish-born husband, who overruled her willingness to allow Collins to drill soldiers on Kilneagh land. As her son recalls, Evie argued that if Collins "ordered assassinations there was justice in what he ordered, for such death was an element in a war that was little different from the war her own countrymen had been waging against the might of the Kaiser" (38). Ironically, as Max Deen Larsen has pointed out,

> The cruel outcome of Eva's faith in militant action is
> captured in the sardonic image of her degradation:
> "what appeared to be a hundred maps of Ireland: the
> trade-mark of Paddy Whiskey on a mass of labels,
> the bottles arrayed like an army on the shelves."
> (1992, 260–1)

After Willie murders Sergeant Rudkin and after his English
cousin/lover Marianne, unbeknownst to him, returns to
Kilneagh to raise their child, violence comes to obsess her.
Marianne's guilt at her own nationality compels her to immerse herself in Irish history, but she does not share Fr
Kilgarriff's revulsion at violence. Despite the priest's remon-
strations, Marianne recounts stories of bloodshed to her
sensitive, imaginative daughter, Imelda, eventually helping to
drive the girl mad.

Trevor frees this Big House novel from established patterns by creating characters who are individuals rather than
types. The Quintons are not the sort of careless, exploita-
tive Ascendancy family so often to be found in this genre.
Anna Quinton, Willie's great-grandmother, died of famine-
fever while caring for the starving and the sick during the
Great Hunger. Before her death she had alienated her English family through her outrage at the mishandling of famine
relief from England. Even after death Anna continues to influence life at Kilneagh: according to legend, she haunted her
grief-stricken husband, urging him to redress some of the
injustice done to the Irish by returning most of the estate to
survivors of the Famine. Whether the apparition existed or
not, her husband fulfilled the request.

Mary Gordon has observed that ". . . up to 1918, Willie's
childhood is that rare thing, happy, and Trevor succeeds in
that rarer thing, portraying a happy childhood convincingly"
(1991, 47–8). Kilneagh is a loving home, a shelter for
vulnerable people. Yet Trevor does not oversentimentalise

Kilneagh, and if its portrayal at times seems idyllic, it must be remembered that Willie is the narrator, recalling a happy childhood now long overshadowed by tragedy. Signs of trouble in Ireland and in the wider world exist but are muted, for naturally the child is often shielded from adult worries. However, even in the adult world Trevor does illustrate how tolerance and compassion are possible. Catholic and Protestant live together harmoniously at Kilneagh. In fact, Willie is unaware of religious bigotry until he attends the school of the sexually predatory, anti-Catholic Miss Halliwell.

Trevor does not gloss over the injustices and brutalities of Irish colonial history, however. Though stories of Irish suffering at the hands of the colonising English figure largely in the child Willie's history lessons, the family's cantankerous gardener is named O'Neill, a subtle reminder on Trevor's part that once-powerful Irish families have been displaced. The Quintons' own privileged lives are rooted in dispossession. Further, as Willie matures, preparing for his role as heir to Kilneagh, he is sent away to be educated in the style of an English gentleman.

Significantly, though, the Quintons are not at home among the Ascendancy. When it becomes known that Willie's parents have supported Michael Collins, they incur the wrath of their neighbours, who view them "as traitors to our class and to the Anglo-Irish tradition" (33); this is a hostility that goes back generations, for historically the Quinton family had long supported Irish independence and opposed English injustice.

Trevor portrays this Ascendancy family sympathetically not to be an apologist for the Anglo-Irish, nor to challenge nationalist narratives of Irish history by engaging in "a revisionist search for an ideal nationalist landlord" (Kreilkamp, 1998: 225), but to demonstrate the horrors wrought by senseless violence. As Andrew Parkin has observed:

> The overall effect of the novel is to celebrate love
> over warfare, healing over bloodshed, reconciliation
> over revenge. It might be thought that Trevor hopes
> to head off class hatred by making the Quintons
> Protestant supporters of Irish Nationalism, and in
> Willie's case capable of carrying out "reprisals". But
> this is legitimate, since historically there were As-
> cendancy supporters of the Irish Cause. (1988, 316)

As Trevor consistently demonstrates in his fiction, acts of
violence are both widely destructive and contagious. So
many lives are maimed by this tragedy, including those of the
survivors.

The forces ranged against non-violence are formidable
here. Willie's beloved friend and teacher Fr Kilgarriff, though
outraged at English injustice, has told the boy that his own
heroes are Anna Quinton and Daniel O'Connell, and that violence is both evil and futile. But Kilgarriff is himself a casualty
of peace: he was defrocked not because of his rumoured love
for a young woman but because she, infatuated with the
priest, was the daughter of a powerful man whose anti-British
feelings clashed with Kilgarriff's pacifism. Similarly, Willie as a
young man seems "to possess the potential for a normal future" (Gordon, 1991: 48); but grief over his mother's death
hurls him into violence. Even the nuns at the school Imelda
attends glorify her father's savage act of revenge against Rudkin, comparing Willie to Cuchulainn and Fionn mac Cumhaill.

Imelda, an imaginative, empathetic child, crumbles mentally under the strain of her knowledge. Curious about her
family, she, like Fogarty in "The News from Ireland", eaves-
drops and pries into hidden documents to discover the secrets that no one will discuss with her. She imagines her
father buying a knife from an elderly shopkeeper; she relives
tragedies old and new: the death of her child aunts, the
murder of Rudkin. And all the while the child battles the

onset of madness by whispering words from Yeats's pastoral "Innisfree" — but violence is victor:

> She searched in her mind for the poetry but she could not remember the order of the words. She closed her eyes and in the room above the vegetable shop blood spurted in a torrent, splashing on to the wallpaper that was torn and hung loosely down. The blood was sticky, running over the backs of her hands and splashing onto her hair.
>
> . . . The screaming of the children began, and the torment of the flames on their flesh. The dogs were laid out dead in the yard, and the body of the man in the teddy-bear dressing-gown lay smouldering on the stairs. (219)

As in "Saints", Willie, who has been living in Italy, returns to Ireland to be at Josephine's deathbed. But the story here takes a different turn: he also eventually goes back to Ireland to live, discovering his child, whom he had never seen, and being reunited with his lost love, now an elderly woman. And it is to Willie's mad daughter Imelda that healing power and saintliness are accorded; madness has forged for her a beautiful world unblighted by the atrocities of real life, and in the final scene of the novel her parents are reunited quietly by the love of their now middle-aged child.

For the Quintons, Trevor offers a final redemption of sorts, but the terms are costly: life stirs in the ashes of murder and despair, but ironically, Imelda is happiest of all (like Ivy in *Mrs Eckdorf in O'Neill's Hotel*) only because her madness spares her from reality and all its suffering. After so many years, the Quintons' love endures: at the novel's quiet close, this now-elderly couple plan to harvest the abundant mulberries from bushes first planted by Anna Quinton. This generous, compassionate, peace-loving woman endures beyond the brutalities of the past.

Fools of Fortune has been rightly praised for its rich evo-
cation of setting, its shocking portrayal of the impact of violence on the vulnerable, its moving conclusion. But the novel
also marks a transitional phase in Trevor's Irish fiction, revealing ambiguous, conflicted attitudes toward the Irish past.

The complex ironies that inform the depictions of the
Anglo-Irish in "The News from Ireland" and *The Silence in
the Garden* and that have early manifestations in "The Distant
Past" are largely absent here, though ironic situations
abound. Though the Quintons are not idealised, as has been
argued above, they are treated somewhat indulgently. They
inspire devotion, not resentment, in their Catholic servants,
who literally lay down their lives for them. Interestingly, the
snobbery and sense of privilege that characterise the narrator of "Saints" are absent from Willie in *Fools of Fortune*. The
Quintons, including the three English women who become
part of the family — Anna, Evie and Marianne — attempt in
some respects to become, if not "more Irish than the Irish",
at least *as* Irish as they.

A notable exception to this attempt at assimilation is
Willie's education. Though as a child he is placed under the
tutelage of Fr Kilgarriff, he is later sent to Miss Halliwell's
school for Protestant children, then to his father's own
boarding school in the Dublin mountains, an institution
complete with not only the traditional English public school
trappings of rugby, cricket, and fagging, but also the inept
teachers, sexually prurient adolescents, and petty cruelties
that characterise Trevor's depiction of English boarding
schools throughout his fiction. Willie does not have to leave
Ireland to acquire an Englishman's education.

Willie's education highlights both his Anglo-Irish identity
and his connection to Marianne, his English cousin. In the
later "The News from Ireland", Mr Pulvertaft is insistent that
his children be taught by an English governess; Mr Quinton is
equally insistent that Willie be educated in the style of an

English gentleman. Willie's two schools underline his separation from Catholic Ireland, for the distasteful Miss Halliwell makes disparaging remarks about Catholics, including describing Fr Kilgarriff, whom she has never met, as "'an uncouth country priest'" (60). Truly deserving of that adjective is the loutish schoolmate who assures Willie that "'Catholic girls are the best for a ride'" (76).

Willie's experiences with the sexually threatening Miss Halliwell and the incompetent teachers at his boarding school align him to Marianne, for after leaving Kilneagh following the funeral of Willie's mother and her subsequent sexual encounter with Willie, she is sexually harassed by her own teacher, the vile Professor Gibb-Bachelor. Willie and Marianne are linked in their vulnerability and their sexual victimisation.

But as with so much of this novel, we teeter between conflicting interpretations. Willie and Marianne, though emotionally compatible, both have personal histories marked by sexual abuse and violence. Further, they are closely related in a family notable for its consanguinity: Anna Quinton and Willie's own mother are both related to Marianne, and both became mistresses of Kilneagh. James Cahalan has speculated that perhaps the mental illness of the couple's daughter, Imelda, may be suggestive "not only of the troubled relationship, or lack of relationship, between her parents, but also of their already interwoven gene pool" (1999, 158). Similarly, Marianne's plaintive and much-quoted observation that the map of England and Ireland resembles embracing lovers may be interpreted as a mournful commentary on the two countries' continuing strife. Yet Thomas Morrissey, despite his deplorable sexual terminology, is surely right in pointing up the irony of this observation:

> The embrace of England and Ireland brings about the
> rise and extinction of the Quintons, the Anglo-Irish

> class traitors who marry English and think Irish. The
> embraces between lovers that have made the Quin-
> ton family possible have occurred, therefore, pre-
> cisely because the English rape of Ireland has made
> them possible. (1990, 60)

Further, the novel's omnisciently narrated opening passages,
describing Kilneagh and Woodcombe Park and providing a
brief history of the Woodcombe–Quinton alliance over several generations, may be variously interpreted. Two harmonious marriages resulted, yet both marriages were shattered
by events at least partly attributable to the English: Anna
Woodcombe Quinton's outrage at the English government's
indifference toward Famine suffering is ended by her own
death from famine-fever; Evie Quinton's ardent support of
Irish nationalism ends in murder and suicide. The final family
romance ends not in marriage but in the melancholy reunion
of two elderly lovers and their mentally deranged child, and
this conclusion, though poignant, is not as emotionally satisfying as some critics have argued. Looked at another way,
the conjunction of England and Ireland through the Woodcombes and the Quintons has been disastrous.

The opening descriptions of Kilneagh and Woodcombe
Park as they appear in the novel's present tense carry the
same sort of duality. Though there may be some comfort in
the survival of these ancestral homes for so many generations,
the differences between their fates are striking. Though
Marianne is descended from the Woodcombes' "poor relations" and thus did not occupy the manor house, her clergyman father benefited from his marriage into the family, for his
wife's relatives controlled the choice of pastor for the town.
Thus, Marianne grew up in the environs of Woodcombe Park.
This sixteenth-century house continues to hang on by its fin-
gernails by becoming a tourist attraction, the family reluctantly tolerating fee-paying visitors in order to survive. In

contrast, Kilneagh remains in ruins, the nearby town of Lough economically depressed and "without attractions" (10). The tenacity of both places may be symbolic of the surviving spirits of the two linked families, but looked at another way, the two houses illustrate the inequities and injustices of Irish history.

In his attempt to demonstrate the futility of violence and the necessity for healing, Trevor enlists both irony and allegory less pointedly than in his later Big House works, but these devices do not disappear completely. When Willie returns to Ireland to see Josephine, for instance, Trevor includes some of the references to Northern Ireland that marked the earlier "Saints". When the cabdriver notes that Cork is "thriving" because the "Yanks love Cork" (224), he adds,

> "There's a few, sir, put off by the trouble up in the North. There's a confusion that we might be affected down here. But there's not so many like that." (224)

Willie echoes the man's unconscious irony by commenting, "'I've read about the trouble'"(224), in one sentence both asserting his detachment from Ireland and refusing to connect his own tragic past with present strife, just as the cabdriver disavows any connection between prosperous Cork and the economically and politically divided North. However, though he retains this subtly ironic exchange, Trevor transforms the Josephine of "Saints", a mentally disturbed woman whose prayers linked the victims of Kilneagh and the victims in Northern Ireland, into a quite sane, religious woman who continues to pray for the victims of Kilneagh. In other words, Trevor mutes the most pointed connection between past and present political strife.

Only three years after the publication of *Fools of Fortune*, Trevor tunnelled further into the Anglo-Irish past. In "The News from Ireland", the saintly Anna Quinton is replaced by the well-meaning but morally blind Pulvertafts, who construct a comfortable *modus vivendi* in the face of disaster. In this work and in the novel that in effect becomes its sequel, *The Silence in the Garden*, Trevor's Big House fiction is transformed into an increasingly allegorical reading of Ireland's colonial history.

"The News from Ireland" (1986), Trevor's brilliant story of the Potato Famine, continues the author's longstanding preoccupation with history's impact on individual lives. But "The News from Ireland" signals a shift in Trevor's historical stance, for in this story he concerns himself, like playwright Brian Friel, with "making history". Whereas in much of his earlier fiction, as Christensen and Pihl have noted, ". . . the lives of his protagonists are determined by what took place in the past" (1989, 207), in "The News from Ireland" the protagonists are not universally caught in the grasp of inexorable historical forces beyond their control; rather, their attitudes and choices shape the course of Irish history, their mistakes join the continuum of injustice wrought by colonial occupation.

"The News from Ireland" must have been percolating in Trevor's imagination as he was writing the non-fiction *A Writer's Ireland: Landscape in Literature* (1984). Echoes of the story's title appear in a passage quoted from John J. O'Meara's translation of Giraldus Cambrensis's twelfth-century *Topographia Hibernica* (*History and Topography of Ireland*). Having declared Ireland reptile-free (and Giraldus numbers toads, frogs and scorpions among the reptiles), Giraldus nevertheless notes the appearance of an ominous frog in Waterford, and quotes King Duvendalus of Ossory's sorrowful reaction: "That reptile brings very bad news to Ireland" (*WI*, 54). In Trevor's story, the news from Ireland is decidedly bleak: the Potato Famine and England's inadequate relief of the suffering wrought by it are but the latest disasters in a country where centuries of invasion and oppression have taken their toll. "The News from Ireland" dissects a sick society in miniature, focusing on one Big House family's increasing detachment from the realities of their adopted country.

Much of Big House literature depicts the estate in decline or on the verge of destruction. Trevor, in contrast, depicts the Pulvertafts in prosperity, their home as a comfortable haven from the horrors that lurk just beyond the gate. Trevor keeps the starving Irish offstage and focuses instead on the denizens of the Big House. Using multiple points of view — the Pulvertaft family, their newly arrived English governess, their estate manager, and their butler — Trevor provides a chilling account of how ignorance, bigotry, and inequality generate disaster.

The Pulvertafts, whose name sounds uncomfortably like "pulverise", are unintentional evildoers. Having inherited a grand estate in Ireland, Mr Pulvertaft convinces himself that his presence will prove beneficial to the Irish. Unconvinced by Pulvertaft's assertion that he feels duty-bound to rescue the land from further decline, the governess, Anna Maria Heddoe, shrewdly thinks to herself that "when Mr Pulvertaft first looked upon drawings of the house and gardens his unexpected inheritance must have seemed like a gift from heaven . . ." (*CS*, 884).

The Pulvertafts respond to the Famine with a mixture of benevolence, ignorance, and indifference. Believing himself to be acting charitably, Pulvertaft employs the starving to construct a road around the estate. In fact, such "famine roads" were an attempt designed by the British government to enable the hungry to earn sustenance, usually by labouring on public works projects. But as Cormac Ó Gráda has noted, after October 1846 ". . . landlords were allowed to sponsor works that would improve their properties, provided they accepted responsibility for all the charges incurred" (1989, 54). In fact, then, Pulvertaft is personally assuming considerable expense because he misguidedly believes that the best way to help the hungry is to give them employment —

employment that matches severely weakened workers and hard physical labour.

Historically, the roadbuilding scheme was both inhumane and a dismal failure as a relief strategy, as the workers' wages did not allow them "to command subsistence at prevailing prices" (Ó Gráda, 54). James Donnelly agrees that ". . . too many earned too little to enable them to ward off starvation and disease" (1989, 302). Trevor makes it clear that Pulvertaft's attempted benevolence is both short-sighted and ineffectual. The futility of the road is symbolically reflected in its circularity. Commenting that when the road is completed it will enhance the aesthetic value of the estate, Pulvertaft complacently observes:

> "Now, what could be nicer . . . than a picnic of lunch by the lake, then a drive through the silver birches, another pause by the abbey, continuing by the river for a mile, and home by Bright Purple Hill? This road, Miss Heddoe, has become my pride." (884)

Congratulating himself on his charity and believing that later generations will remember him for the road — a belief laden with irony, for the road will eventually be overgrown and the road-building project bitterly resented for in effect denying charity to the suffering — he fails to see, as even his hard-bitten estate manager does, that the workers are too physically debilitated to lift heavy boulders or, as his butler, Fogarty, observes to Miss Heddoe, that this road "'that leads nowhere'" "'only insults the pride of the men who built it . . .'" (903). Having been assured by the Distress Board that he has relieved the suffering, Pulvertaft sees nothing incongruous in his placid observation, in noting how many of the surviving Irish are emigrating to America, that "'At least . . . there is somewhere for them to go'" (901).

Mrs Pulvertaft's conscience is more troubled, though her anxiety manifests itself primarily in dreams. Her contribution to the relief effort is her distribution of soup to the hungry, and she accepts the word of male authority — her husband, her minister and the British government — that nothing more can be done. In her waking life, Mrs Pulvertaft accepts Rev. Poole's belief that the Famine is a sign of God's wrath, her husband's self-congratulatory conviction that the road is beneficial, and her government's assurance that more aggressive famine relief would destroy the English economy. But Mrs Pulvertaft's dreams belie her waking life. She dreams of running naked on the seashore freed from the constraints of Victorian social convention. In another telling dream, Rev. Poole exhorts the congregation to wash the feet of Jesus, and, believing that Jesus is one of the Irish road workers, Mrs Pulvertaft approaches the work crew, only to be rejected.

The Pulvertaft children, whose futures are the abiding concern of Mrs Pulvertaft's life, remain largely untouched by the Famine. Charlotte, pretty and superficial, resigns herself to marrying an Anglo-Irish soldier, naïvely reflecting that "it probably will be nice, knowing devotion like this for ever" (899). Adelaide, whose plainness deems her unmarriageable in the eyes of her family, remains oblivious to the Famine, consumed as she is with unrequited love for her sister's fiancé. Emily, whose restlessness to travel is rooted in her reluctance to assume her expected social role as a husband's wife or a brother's dependent, does in fact love Ireland, albeit a romanticised image of the country. Enamoured of the monastic ruins on the Pulvertaft estate, Emily idealises Ireland's past and ignores its terrible present.

Among the siblings, only George Arthur, the youngest Pulvertaft and the heir to the estate, thinks about the Famine. Though still a child, George Arthur slowly acknowledges that his dream of a military career must be sacrificed to his duties as heir to the estate. George Arthur asks his governess whether the Irish "'eat their babies, like in the South Seas'", unconsciously invoking Swift's "A Modest Proposal" — a connection that is surely deliberate, as Swift is mentioned several times within the story as having been a former visitor to the estate. The Anglo-Irish Dean seems to have been likewise a despoiling visitor, for family lore has it that he ordered the felling of elm trees to improve the view (895).

Trevor emphasises that the Pulvertafts, eight-year denizens of Ireland, "make allowances for the natives, they come to terms, they learn to live with things" (881). Seduced by a rich inheritance, lulled into complacency by their comfortable lives, the Pulvertafts have allowed their moral sensibilities to become blunted. Not inherently evil — as Fogarty puts it, "'The wickedness here is not intentional'" (904) — the Pulvertafts suffer from the serious sin of *accidia*.

Protestant and poor, Fogarty belongs neither to the privileged lives of the Anglo-Irish nor to the miserable existence of the impoverished Catholics. His role as outsider aligns him with Trevor himself, who has observed in his memoirs:

> I was fortunate that my accident of birth actually placed me on the edge of things. I was born into a minority that all my life has seemed in danger of withering away. This was smalltime Protestant stock, far removed from the well-to-do Ascendancy of the recent past but without much of a place in de Valera's new Catholic Ireland. (*ERW*, xiii)

Fogarty could in fact be Trevor's imaginary ancestor, for as he describes himself and his sister: "Poor Irish Protestants as they were, he and his sister belonged neither outside the estate gates with the people who had starved nor with a family as renowned as the Pulvertafts" (905).

Observing the inequities between the Pulvertafts' comfortable lives and the sufferings of their tenants, Fogarty clings to the ultimately disappointed hope that Miss Heddoe, troubled as she is by the horrors of the Famine, will speak up to their employers in a way that he cannot. Fogarty, who evinces an acute understanding of Irish history, wishes to halt the cycle of invasion and oppression, and believes that the newly arrived Heddoe will not succumb to their employers' complacency.

Eccentric and, as Robert Rhodes has observed, "more than a little sinister, moving always in secrecy and penetrating the secrets of others while husbanding his own" (1989, 40), Fogarty becomes obsessed with Heddoe, secretly reading her diary and letters, unrealistically placing upon her the burden of enlightening the Pulvertafts and in effect changing the course of Irish history.

In Anna Maria Heddoe, Trevor provides a sensitive portrait of that most distressful of Victorian women, the governess. Lonely, bewildered by her employers' limited sympathy for the suffering Irish, Heddoe pours into her diary her private incomprehension and anxiety. She is reminiscent of Albert Memmi's description of the "new arrival" who is as yet unaccustomed to life in a colony. The new arrival is shocked at poverty and injustice, horrified at the colonials' indifference, and wants to return home as soon as possible. Yet sometimes, like Anna Maria Heddoe, the "new arrival" is committed to stay by employment, and thus "liable to get used to the poverty and the rest" (Memmi, 1965: 19).

Fogarty rightly assumes that she is still capable of being exercised by injustice, horrified by suffering, as her employers are no longer capable of being. When Fogarty relates that a poor family's child has been marked with stigmata, the governess is shocked at the Pulvertafts' assumption that the wounds have been inflicted by the parents, and confides to her diary, "I wept before I went to bed. I wept again when I lay there, hating more than ever the place I am in, where people are driven back to savagery" (897).

The stigmatised child, of whom Kristin Morrison has asserted, ". . . the child is clearly an emblem of the peasantry itself, crucified by the ascendancy, the poor crucified by the rich" (1993, 12), in fact illustrates the gulf between Heddoe and her employers. When Fogarty first informs the governess of the child's existence, she is willing to accept a miraculous explanation, and cannot understand why the Pulvertafts have made no mention of the event. She naïvely wonders why such an astounding occurrence does not find its way into the family conversation.

When Fogarty later assures her that he and the Pulvertafts have concluded that the wounds were inflicted by the parents, Heddoe is horrified. Fogarty's own anti-Catholic bias leads him to assert that the child's wounds were a hoax fostered by a drunken priest. Heddoe for her part wants to believe in a miraculous explanation. But Fogarty's response silences and shocks her: the family in question had already suffered the deaths of seven children and four grandparents; only the parents and the baby remain alive. Fogarty shares with Heddoe his sister's conviction that the wounds were inflicted in a desperate attempt to halt annihilation. After the baby dies, Heddoe is tormented by her imaginings of the family's suffering as well as the Pulvertafts' reticence about the event.

Yet sensitive and sympathetic as she is, Anna Maria Heddoe cannot realise Fogarty's hopes that the cycle of invasion and usurpation can be broken in Ireland. She depends upon the Pulvertafts for her livelihood and has already compromised herself. When the family pretends that plain daughter Adelaide can compensate for her lack of beauty with her musical accomplishment, Heddoe dishonestly praises the young woman's clumsy piano playing. Further, she is inevitably conditioned by her English upbringing. She assumes that the Famine is a manifestation of God's displeasure, and her God apparently views the English as His chosen people:

> . . . I wonder — for I cannot help it — what in His
> name these people have done to displease God so? It
> is true they have not been an easy people to govern
> . . . their superstitious worship is a sin. But God is a
> forgiving God. I pray to understand His will. (900)

Heddoe also unwittingly perpetuates injustice, for responsible as she is for the education of George Arthur, the son and heir, she unquestioningly teaches him from a history text that rationalises an earlier act of English aggression, the dissolution of the monasteries during the reign of Henry VIII.

Miss Heddoe's complicity in the historical process is sealed when she decides to marry Erskine, the Pulvertafts' callous estate manager, whose "temper is short, his disposition unsentimental, his soldier's manner abrupt; nor is there, beneath that vigorous exterior, a gentler core" (891). He believes the Famine is "ill fortune", just as his loss of an arm is the ill fortune that ended his military career. Distrustful of the Irish, contemptuous of his employer, who in his eyes is a "painless inheritor" who "takes too easily for granted the good fortune that came his way" (891), Erskine spares pity neither for himself nor for the road-workers he supervises. By marrying him, Heddoe aligns herself with the Pulvertafts and other invaders.

Fogarty sadly concedes, "Stranger and visitor, she has learnt to live with things" (906): as the estate manager's wife, she will indeed become one of the "strangers" with a stake in maintaining the status quo of English occupation. She, like the Pulvertafts, has been seduced by comfort. Though she does not love Erskine, marrying him will elevate her social status. And considering her continuing economic dependence on the Pulvertafts — for, after all, they employ Erskine — it is unlikely that the sentiments of dismay and incomprehension that fill her diary will ever find their way to the family's ears.

In "The News from Ireland", those who suffer the ravages of hunger and disease are kept at a distance. Though we hear the rumours of the stigmatised child and are made privy to Mrs Pulvertaft's dreams and Miss Heddoe's diary entries, both haunted by the faces of the starving women who come to the estate seeking food, to a large extent we are as insulated as the Pulvertafts from the physical horrors of the Famine. Instead, Trevor uses hunger as a metaphor to depict the disastrous potato famine not as a "tragic ecological accident" (Ó Gráda, 1989: 76), not as an English act of genocide, but rather as a profound failure of the human community.

Just as physical starvation plagues the Irish poor, emotional hunger gnaws beneath the placid surface of the Pulvertaft household. Notably absent from the genteel conversation of the drawing-room is any mention of Adelaide's unhappiness, Emily's frustration at women's limited opportunities, Charlotte's half-hearted marriage, George Arthur's disappointed hopes. Mrs Pulvertaft keeps her unhappy dreams to herself; Erskine conceals his wounded pride beneath a gruff exterior; Miss Heddoe confides her heartache only to her diary.

These emotionally hungry characters lack nothing in the way of physical nourishment. As Robert Rhodes has noted, "Trevor ironically limns starvation without by repletion within . . ." (1989, 40). In the midst of this plenty, however, linger signs that the well-nourished are ill at ease with their good fortune. While families starve on the estate, stout Mrs Pulvertaft suffers from daily bouts of indigestion. Though her overindulgence is a disturbing reminder of how removed the Anglo-Irish are from the grim realities of the Famine, the indigestion may be indicative of her uneasy conscience.

Similarly, Miss Heddoe's delicate stomach cannot tolerate the food prepared by Fogarty's sister, and like the Irish, with whom she sympathises, she grows thinner. Yet she thoughtlessly wastes food while others starve. Ultimately, the starved bodies of the Irish and the hungry hearts of the Big House remain unassuaged. Decimated families, loveless marriages, disappointed hopes: these are the legacy of the Famine, and by the end of the story there are ominous hints of its consequences. Fogarty predicts a future in which the Pulvertaft dominion crumbles. Implying that "the descendants of the people who were hungry" will exact retribution, Fogarty reveals to Miss Heddoe that his dreams have foretold the murder of George Arthur's son and the family's subsequent abandonment of the house, the overgrowing of the famine road. He also describes an arson fire at the estate manager's house and the consequent deaths of the unspecified inhabitants. Surely this last has personal meaning for Heddoe: does Fogarty foretell her own death, the deaths of her husband and children? But Miss Heddoe, frightened and repelled by Fogarty's disturbing confidences, rejects him.

Gregory Schirmer has argued that the "governing moral force" in Trevor's fiction is "the tension between Forster's 'Only Connect' and Eliot's 'I can connect / nothing with nothing'" (1990, 1): that is, "the complex vision of contemporary life generated by both an advocacy of Forster's principle of compassion and connection and a counterpointing, realistic assessment of contemporary society as alienated and disconnected" (2). "The News from Ireland" shares Trevor's earlier preoccupation with the failure of human relationships; yet it also evinces the increasing separateness of Trevor's Irish works from his fiction with English or other European settings, a growing preoccupation with Ireland's colonial legacy. In Fogarty, the perceptive yet ultimately impotent butler, Trevor focuses his own complex vision of Ireland.

Unlike his employers, Fogarty is acutely aware of history and cognisant that the Famine will have profound and far-reaching consequences. Classifying the Pulvertafts with other past "visitors", Fogarty wishes to stem the tide of invasion:

> Fogarty is an educated man, and thinks of other visitors there have been: the Celts, whose ramshackle gypsy empire expired in this same landscape, St Patrick with his holy shamrock, the outrageous Vikings preceding the wily Normans, the adventurers of the Virgin Queen. His present employers arrived here also, eight years ago, in 1839. . . . He does not dislike the Pulvertafts of Ipswich, he has nothing against them beyond the fact that they did not stay where they were. (881)

The passage is fraught with irony, as the "educated" Fogarty well knows, for the aforementioned "visitors" *stayed*, had a profound, often violent impact on Irish history. One cannot help but wonder how the Pulvertafts of Ipswich, placed as they are in such company, will be remembered in future generations.

Fogarty's dearest wish is to see Ireland in the literal sense de-colonised: he dreams that the estate, symbolic of Ireland itself, will decline "back into the clay it came from", all signs of foreign occupation erased. Obsessed though he is with Miss Heddoe, he hopes she will leave Ireland, that her "sharp fresh eye", having "needled out" the "wickedness" of dispossession, will compel her to refuse to "learn to live with things", to refuse to become complicit in Ireland's occupation and exploitation. For though his own eye is no longer "fresh", it has "needled out" the Pulvertafts' private thoughts, and having unscrupulously read Miss Heddoe's letters and diary, he knows her most intimate thoughts as well. Asserting that he is "no humanitarian", Fogarty calmly asserts that the place is full of "wickedness", that the estate should have been left to decline, its fruit trees and game become the sustenance of the hungry: "'The past would have withered away, miss. Instead of which it is the future that's withering now'" (904).

Despite Fogarty's oddity and the reductiveness of his solution for Ireland's ills, it is clear that Trevor invests him with a certain moral authority in the story: he is one of Trevor's "truth-tellers" (Gitzen, 1979), characters who bring to light uncomfortable truths, for which acts of honesty they are usually ignored or ostracised. Like Cynthia in "Beyond the Pale", "Attracta", Ivy Eckdorf and others, Fogarty attempts to jolt his listener into an awareness of her own self-delusion and unwitting complicity in injustice. Like them, he is a flawed prophet whose own eccentricity guarantees that he will not be taken seriously. It is difficult to accept Gregory Schirmer's dismissal of Fogarty as "fanatical", a "figure of alienation and disconnection" (1990, 146) who cannot accept the Pulvertafts, "no matter what their motives and what they do to try to relieve the suffering of their starving tenants" simply "because they are not Irish" (146).

Fogarty's message is rejected, for when he confides in Miss Heddoe, she accuses him of drunkenness and threatens to complain to Pulvertaft, despite the fact that the butler has voiced her own secret sentiments of shock and outrage at the treatment of the Irish. His earlier wish that Miss Heddoe would speak up is quashed, and realising his inability to sway her, Fogarty resigns himself to silence.

Perceiving painful truths and telling them are usually mutually exclusive in this story. Fogarty and Heddoe, the two most perceptive characters, are, respectively, silenced and silent, their private news from Ireland buried. Robert Rhodes wonders, ". . . why would Fogarty the butler in 'News' not tell all that he might and why does Anna Maria Heddoe abort the search for the truth?" (1989, 49); yet considering the characters' circumstances, is their silence so surprising? Fogarty and Heddoe are servants whose livelihood depends on the good will of the Pulvertafts. As a governess,

Heddoe occupies a place socially superior to Fogarty, but she is still essentially powerless. Were she to "smack out" her private beliefs about the Pulvertafts' moral lapses in the face of the Famine, she would just as surely be dismissed as would Fogarty for similar behaviour. Ultimately, Heddoe's choice of learning "to live with things" necessitates that she "abort her search for the truth": though marriage to Erskine will elevate her socially, Heddoe is still confined by her status as a Victorian woman. Distancing herself from the suffering Irish may be an act of psychological survival; further, it is likely that her future husband, a forceful, narrow-minded man who dislikes the Irish, "intends to permit" as little "nonsense" from a woman as he would from the road-workers he distrusts. One can hardly imagine that Erskine would encourage Heddoe's sympathy for the Irish.

With Heddoe's defection, Fogarty is left alone with his conviction that "'There is wickedness here . . .'" (903), and his assertion is difficult to refute. Beneath the genteel benevolence of the Pulvertaft estate lie starvation, dishonesty, usurpation of land and power, exploitation of the powerless, and a host of other evils. In his religious bigotry and invasion of the governess's privacy, Fogarty is indeed a flawed prophet, but he is a shrewd seer of the news from Ireland — past, present and future — nonetheless.

Indeed, Fogarty's character marks a turning point in Trevor's Irish fiction. Though in his earlier works dealing with Irish political violence and colonial oppression — the short stories "Beyond the Pale", "Attracta", et al. and the novel *Fools of Fortune* — Trevor clearly connects injustice and violence and emphasises both violence's contagion and its futility, in "The News from Ireland" he plumbs Ireland's past more deeply, couching individual lives in the more far-reaching realm of historical allegory.

The story's title is itself indicative of Trevor's scope: he will undertake to convey the news *from Ireland*, not simply the news from a lonely governess or a brooding butler or a well-meaning but ignorant Anglo-Irish family.

The indeterminate setting of the story also encourages a symbolic reading. Trevor, who in other works reveals a delight in Irish placenames and their meanings, recalling the *dinnseanchas* tradition in early Irish literature shared by such contemporary writers as Seamus Heaney and Brian Friel, is markedly silent about the Pulvertaft estate's locale. Unlike other Big Houses in life and literature, including Trevor's own works, the estate has no name. This deliberate ambiguity would seem to suggest that the story's news is indeed from *Ireland*, not from a single estate or a single Anglo-Irish family. Even the colour scheme of the Pulvertafts' drawing-room — white, green and apricot — prefigures the tricolour Irish flag.

Furthermore, Trevor's frequent references to history urge us to place the story in a larger context. Fogarty, who shares his author's interest in history, connects the Pulvertafts to the earlier invaders of Ireland. He does not wish to see history repeat itself, no matter how well-meaning the invaders.

In "The News from Ireland", Trevor evinces his growing concern with, to borrow John Wilson Foster's term, "colonial consequences". Pulvertaft, an inherently kindly man, allows himself to be seduced by his inheritance of an Irish estate, burying the issue of ownership and usurpation beneath a "white man's burden" attitude toward the Irish. If one can insulate oneself from the horrors of the Famine — and Rhodes has noted how Trevor's use of walls, shutters, and other devices symbolises the family's detachment from the suffering without (1989, 39) — life on the Pulvertaft estate can be quite pleasant, with plentiful food, scenic rides, an elegant household. Plied with such temptations, it is perhaps not surprising that the Pulvertafts, like so many other colonials, let "surprise and dismay fade from their faces"

(880); "They make allowances for the natives, they come to terms, they learn to live with things" (880).

Bewildered, frightened, and appalled as she initially is by her news from Ireland, Miss Heddoe also allows herself to be seduced: Erskine can offer her the companionship and financial security lacking in her life as a governess. She, too, as Fogarty observes, "has learnt to live with things" — one of the most tragic statements that Trevor has ever written. When she takes her place in Erskine's house, its garden "'reclaimed . . . as the estate was reclaimed'" (901), she will unintentionally conspire on a smaller scale in the Pulvertafts' dispossession of the Irish.

Neither Miss Heddoe nor the Pulvertafts will fulfil Fogarty's dearest wish by returning to England, nor does it seem that the coming generation will alter the course of Ireland's colonial history. Even as a child, George Arthur betrays the arrogance of the privileged: as he questions Miss Heddoe about cannibalism, he imitates his father's behaviour by blocking the hearth with his body, thus appropriating the fire's warmth for himself and selfishly leaving Miss Heddoe to suffer the cold: already the master/servant roles have become entrenched in the boy's behaviour. George Arthur's dreams of a military career, thwarted by his duties as heir to the estate, reveal how even a child has internalised British colonial attitudes. He longs to go to India as a British soldier, a dream frequently assailed by his sister Emily's assertions that India is a place of disease-bearing flies, polluted water, and uncomfortable barracks — besides, she reminds him, he has his responsibilities as heir. It is clear that neither one of them has ever been encouraged to question why the British army is in India at all; nor do the Indian people figure in the conversation: like the Irish, they have become tangential in their own country.

Trevor neither demonises the Pulvertafts nor suggests that they can single-handedly alter the course of Irish history.

Yet by keeping the story's locale indeterminate and by investing the prophetic Fogarty with his author's own awareness of history and its consequences, Trevor renders "The News from Ireland" an acute appraisal of the effects of England's presence in Ireland: the colonials are not inherently evil, but corrupted by power and susceptible to greed. Both the Pulvertafts and Anna Maria Heddoe become desensitised to the suffering around them because its horrors are almost as unbearable as acknowledging the ugly truth that their own presence in Ireland perpetuates the historical process of dispossession.

In 1988, two years after the publication of "The News from Ireland", Trevor produced the acclaimed novel *The Silence in the Garden*, which likewise exposes the evils of British colonialism through another well-intentioned but destructive family, the Rollestons. In fact, *The Silence in the Garden* is in effect a sequel to "The News from Ireland". Here, too, are multiple points of view, including a governess's diary. Here, too, injustice and moral blindness breed disaster. But in *The Silence in the Garden*, Fogarty's wish is at least partially fulfilled: the Big House family dies without heirs, its once-great estate is "returned . . . to its clay" (*SG*, 204), language that echoes Fogarty's desire that "He and his sister might alone have attended the mouldering of the place, urging it back to the clay" (*CS*, 881–2).

The novel is a microcosm of Irish history. Its setting is an island, Carriglas, whose name means "green rock" (15). Among its landmarks are standing stones, a ruined abbey, a holy well, a Big House. Fogarty's world lingers as well: ancestors of the present Rollestons are remembered for their philanthropy during the Great Hunger. Mrs Rolleston died of famine fever contracted while she was caring for the poor; after the Famine subsided, the family waived rents and tithes to those who survived. In the lifetimes of the central characters of the novel — the early 1900s to the 1970s — Ireland moves from colonial possession to independent republic; Carriglas declines from an elegant Big House to a decaying estate; children learn the Irish language in school; an Ascendancy family expires, and the future is left to the rising Catholics. As Kristin Morrison has observed:

> This fertile green island is Ireland in miniature, a little Emerald Isle in which the whole history of Ireland is played out, from ancient standing stones to holy well, with four lost fields, a decaying estate, a silent garden. (1991, 123)

Like the Pulvertafts, the Rollestons are not inherently evil people, but years of privilege and detachment have blunted their humanity. The decline of their estate is due not only to the passing of an era but also to the festering effects of a long-hidden act of violence. The Rolleston children, Villana, John James, and Lionel, and their cousin Hugh Pollexfen tormented a local child, Corny Dowley, chasing him with their father's shotgun, like hunters with small prey. They are severely reprimanded for this monstrous prank, yet do not heed their elders' commands not to do it again. Years later, Corny Dowley, now fighting in the Irish Civil War, plans a private act of vengeance, but the blast he intends for the Rollestons instead kills the family butler, Linchy.

A cruel, childish prank blights numerous lives. Linchy's fiancée, Brigid, is pregnant, and their child, Tom, suffers in a society that stigmatises illegitimacy. Corny Dowley, who has become a violent man, is hunted and killed by the Black and Tans, and his distraught mother kills herself. Ridden with a guilt they never discuss, the Rolleston siblings, now grown to adulthood, deliberately end the family line. Hugh Pollexfen breaks his engagement to Villana, who eventually enters into a loveless, intentionally childless marriage to an elderly solicitor, Finnamore Balt. John James, once the pride of the family, engages in an embarrassing long-term affair with the rather vulgar Mrs Moledy, a boarding-house owner who is probably no longer of childbearing age. Lionel weds himself to the land and remains wilfully oblivious to the fact that Sarah Pollexfen, the former governess and Hugh's sister, loves him.

In the 1970s, after the Rollestons and Sarah have died, the now-crumbling estate is left to Tom, in acknowledgement of how the family has unwittingly blighted his life. Finally, Tom, whose past has left him feeling unlovable and ashamed, decides he will never marry: strangely lacking in bitterness toward the Rolleston family, he decides to live out the rest of his life at the much-dilapidated Carriglas, making no effort to reverse the process of decay and dissolution.

As in "The News from Ireland", silence, secrecy and a refusal to confront the truth poison human relationships in *The Silence in the Garden*. Just as the Pulvertafts conceal their private disappointments and refuse to confront the harsh realities of life outside their comfortable house, the Rollestons live self-contained and truth-denying lives. Mrs Rolleston, the children's grandmother and one of many wise, elderly, and powerless women who frequent Trevor's fiction, realises too late the disaster wrought by concealing the truth about Corny Dowley and her grandchildren. The child Tom must hear his father's killer lauded as a national hero; the Pollexfen children's masochistic attempts to expiate their guilt are ultimately pointless. Mrs Rolleston herself arrives at the terrible conviction that Corny Dowley, cruel slaughterer and cruelly slaughtered, embraced a violent life not primarily because of his political beliefs but because he was tortured by her thoughtless, privileged grandchildren. She agonises, "'What monstrousness was bred in him that summer, Sarah? . . . How convenient revolution is for men like Cornelius Dowley! What balm for the bitter heart!'" (185–6). What she does not seem to realise is that Carriglas's *malaise* pre-dates her grandchildren, and is rooted in the fact that centuries earlier, the Rollestons, as Fogarty observed of the Pulvertafts, "did not stay where they were" (CS, 881).

Further, her contention that in another place and time her grandchildren "would have escaped their conscience" and "grown up healthily to exorcise their aberrations by shrugging them away" (187) is neither convincing nor morally acceptable, for the Rolleston children's transgressions are bred of the power and privilege they enjoy. When Mrs Rolleston too late unburdens her troubled conscience, she chooses Sarah Pollexfen as her reluctant confessor. Sarah's diary becomes the repository of painful secrets, and before her death she shares them with Tom and the only remaining family servant, Patty.

This revelation on Sarah's part marks a departure from "The News from Ireland". Miss Heddoe, the Pulvertafts' governess, had likewise confided painful feelings to her diary. But Miss Heddoe flees from the truth: shocked and troubled as she is by the unassuaged suffering around her and the indifference of her employers, she eventually learns "to live with things", keeping silent about injustice and marrying a man who despises the Irish. Sarah Pollexfen, in contrast, courageously shares her diary with Tom and Patty, making them privy to her most intimate secrets: her unrequited love for Lionel Rolleston, her inability to halt the Rolleston children's savagery, her own past evasion of the truth. But Sarah Pollexfen, like Mrs Rolleston, is powerless to change the past, however she may deplore it.

Sarah's relationship with the Rollestons is also complicated by the fact that she is related to them by blood, her employment an act of charity on their part. Unlike Miss Heddoe, who is bewildered and repulsed by her new surroundings, Sarah Pollexfen cannot believe her good fortune. She first arrives at Carriglas in 1908 to be governess to Villana Rolleston; when a matured Villana no longer needs

her, Sarah embarks on years of quiet desperation, first as a
teacher at the tedious Misses Goodbody's School for Protestant Girls, then as her father's housekeeper at Dunadry
Rectory. Her father, a scholar studying the Book of Ruth, is
so entranced with a Biblical daughter that he cruelly neglects
his own. In fact, as Max Deen Larsen observes, Sarah's life
mimics Ruth's, for she, too, "devotes her life to an adopted
family in a distant land" (1992, 268) — or, at least, in a distant part of Ireland. As Sarah reflects, "I believe I might cut
my hair down to the roots and still he would not comment"
(23). She has never forgotten his dismissive comment when
she was a child: "'A pity there's no prettiness in her'" (23).

Unlike Miss Heddoe, who as an English woman views
Ireland as an alien place, Sarah Pollexfen is one of the "poor
Irish Protestants" who occupy much of Trevor's fiction, and
the Misses Goodbody's School provides yet another microcosm of Ireland:

> Thirty-five Protestant girls at a time grow through
> their difficult years at the Misses Goodbody's: daugh-
> ters of hardware merchants and coal merchants, of
> bank managers and grocers, farmers' daughters and
> drapers' daughters, clergyman's daughters at re-
> duced fees. "Tenants of a landless empire," one of
> them colourfully remarks. "We are the Jews of Ire-
> land." (20)

Sarah, who shares a surname with W.B. Yeats's mother,
must serve the bourgeoisie, the echelon of Irish society that
Yeats despised.

Memories of Carriglas have sustained Sarah through her
unhappy years at Misses Goodbody's School and Dunadry
Rectory, and when after her father's death in 1931 Sarah is
invited to return to the Rollestons, the prospect is at first a
Paradise found. Yet from the beginning, one senses the
shadows in Sarah's dream place: unlike her brother, who is

treated as an equal by the Rollestons, even becoming engaged to Villana, the only daughter, Sarah is treated as a dependant: the Rollestons' charity has rescued her from
poverty, and she must earn her keep. In this novel that
blends omniscient narrative and first-person diary entries, as
does "The News from Ireland", Sarah is often absent from
the narrative, reflecting her marginal presence in the household. One of the very few times that Sarah is mentioned
outside of her diary is when John James's mistress, Mrs
Moledy, having imbibed too much whiskey at Villana's wedding, fuzzily discerns a "serious-faced little creature" (145)
— one thinks of Jane Eyre — then decides it must be "the
female who'd been hanging about the place for years, some
type of poor relation" (145). When another wedding guest
fails to speak to her, Sarah speculates that the woman does
not want to acknowledge that she may be distantly related
to a household dependant.

Although at first her return to Carriglas seems the ful-
filment of a dream, Sarah comes to share Miss Heddoe's
bewilderment. In the years intervening between her first
visit to Carriglas and her return, the children's father has
been killed in the First World War, partial Irish independence has been achieved, and civil war has raged. Villana and
Hugh have become first engaged then estranged, Linchy is
murdered, Tom has been born, and Mrs Rolleston is dying.
The once-happy household has become a melancholy place.
When Villana's marriage to Finnamore Balt approaches,
Sarah reflects, "I feel more than ever that I live in a cobweb
of other people's lives and do not understand the cobweb's
nature" (116). The children she once loved have become
thwarted adults, their close affection replaced by strained
distance. Sarah is puzzled and pained by the transformation,
but does not yet fully understand it, bitterly reflecting, "I am
not worthy of whatever secret there is, only good for the
chores a poor relation must take on as her due" (116).

Again, like Miss Heddoe, she feels the desire to flee, but "cannot find the courage" (116). Miss Heddoe will allow her conscience to become numbed and will marry Erskine; Miss Pollexfen will for many years shut her eyes on the secrets of the past so that she may continue to live at Carriglas, confiding her pain only to her diaries.

As is true of much of Trevor's fiction, *The Silence in the Garden* depicts characters entrapped by history and making impotent attempts to grapple with its burden. Finnamore Balt, Villana's unlikely choice of husband, is ignorant of the Rolleston family skeletons, and clings to an ill-advised plan to restore Carriglas to its former prosperity by reacquiring the lands and rents that were surrendered in the post-Famine years. In a chilling echo of Ireland's past, he even contemplates eviction. He cannot comprehend why the Rollestons so vehemently oppose his schemes, why they will not attempt to rescue their decaying estate. Devastatingly ironic is his obsession with reclaiming four fields once possessed by the Rollestons, oblivious as he is to the highly charged nationalist symbolism of four fields, signifying the four provinces of Ireland.

In contrast, the Rolleston siblings' enslavement to the past manifests itself in a futile, perverse attempt at atonement. They pay for their early cruelty by essentially annihilating their family. Life and love are forever blighted for them, and they remain together at Carriglas in uneasy, perpetual guilt, tied to the place by their sense of wrongdoing. Sarah's brother, Hugh, is likewise consumed with guilt. Not only will he not marry Villana, whom he loves, he becomes estranged from his beloved sister because her association with Carriglas is too painful. However, Hugh, although a blood relation of the Rollestons, is able to salvage his life after Carriglas, for he marries and has children. To do so, however, he must leave Ireland. As Kristin Morrison notes,

> Only by leaving Ireland has he been able, apparently,
> to avoid the consequences of his early participation
> in evil; he has cut his ties to his homeland, to his
> family, to his own past. (1991, 71)

Even in their self-inflicted punishment, the Rolleston children retain the self-absorption that their social status has granted them. For though they are guilt-ridden about the tragedy their thoughtless cruelty has provoked, that guilt is self-indulgent, masochism rather than true atonement.

Though Tom and his mother continue to live at Carriglas, only Mrs Rolleston shows any real concern for the lonely child. Villana spends her time reading romance novels and smoking. With his characteristic gift for investing the sometime mundaneness of popular culture with symbolic appropriateness, Trevor concocts romance titles that speak to the Rollestons' predicament, e.g. *Darkened Rooms* and *Out of the Ruins* (177–8). When she agrees to marry Finnamore Balt, it must be on her terms: he must dismiss his loyal housekeeper, abandon his familiar home, even leave behind his cherished cat. Most important of all, he must concede to her insistence that theirs will be a childless marriage. Unlike Villana di Botti, the fourteenth-century Florentine saint for whom she is perhaps named, Villana Rolleston does not turn to active goodness as atonement for her past failings.

John James's Catholic mistress may be absurd, but the contempt with which he treats her is reprehensible. Despite an irritating insistence on female Irish stereotypes that Trevor himself is often at great pains to undermine, Max Deen Larsen's argument that John James, the Anglo-Irish landlord, "wants to enjoy the substance of the native Catholic mother, but certainly not to unite their flesh in marriage" (1992, 272) has some validity. Although he believes that Mrs Moledy is his social inferior, despite his self-loathing after their sexual liaisons, John James continues his visits to her boarding house, the Rose of Tralee, its name suggesting an ironic contrast between the sentimental romantic song and the banal affair. Absorbed as he is in his sexual need, a perverse attempt at self-punishment, John James ignores the fact that Mrs Moledy is a human being and that, preposterous as she is, she genuinely loves him.

Lionel, a gentle, vulnerable, rather weak-willed man, is the least offensive of the Rolleston siblings, yet he nevertheless surrenders some of his humanity. By marrying himself to the land and denying himself Sarah's love, he slips into a half-life. And though he differs from his siblings in that he attempts to live a useful life, he cannot ultimately preserve Carriglas from disintegration. Most of the land must be sold off because Lionel is physically and economically unable to sustain it. In a sense, Lionel selects a far less distasteful species of self-punishing class levelling than does John James: he works alongside the servants, ploughing the fields, attempting to fix the increasingly dilapidated house, etc.

Each of these attempts to deal with their guilt is, however, finally pointless. The Rolleston children lead thwarted lives, and their repentance seems to have taught them little except suffering. One is reminded in contrast of Mr Devereux and Geraldine Carey in "Attracta", who seek atonement for the accidental killing of Attracta's parents by loving and caring for the orphaned girl.

And yet, there is historical appropriateness to the Rollestons' fates. Trevor relates that the family acquired their estate at the time of Cromwell, driving the original owners "to the stony wastes of Mayo" (41). Though many of the Rollestons have been well-meaning, even benevolent, they are part of Fogarty's "invaders". It is symbolically fitting that a bridge eventually connects Carriglas Island with the mainland, for an era is ending, the detachment and privilege of families such as the Rollestons no longer possible.

Trevor suggests in *The Silence in the Garden* that the injustice wrought by colonial occupation thwarts and poisons everyone and everything it touches. Carriglas, an Ireland in miniature, embodies the injustices of the past. Cornelius Dowley, who seems a pathetic, brutal man warped by the poverty and injustice of his early life, is held up as a political martyr, and the bridge that connects Carriglas to the mainland bears his name. And though Mrs Rolleston may attribute Dowley's political violence to her grandchildren's cruelty, the fact of the matter remains that Dowley's poverty, his violence, and his death at the hands of the Black and Tans are part of a long legacy of colonialism.

Trevor explores this legacy not only through the stories of Dowley and the Rollestons, but also through wry observations of the society spawned in the wake of colonialism. The year 1931, a crucial one in the novel, marks both the building of the Cornelius Dowley Bridge and the marriage of Villana Rolleston. With devastating humour, Trevor describes the cast of Anglo-Irish eccentrics assembled for the wedding. John James's Catholic mistress, Mrs Moledy, shatters their composure by arriving uninvited, imbibing the better portion of a bottle of whiskey, and alarming the Bishop of Killaloe with her chumminess.

Like Mrs Moledy, the community's Catholics, though possessing more vitality than their Protestant neighbours, are likewise unimpressive, notably for their hypocrisy. Throughout his childhood, Tom is cruelly stigmatised because of his illegitimacy. "Holy" Mullihan, an unpleasant schoolboy aspiring to the priesthood, piously points out to Tom that his birth was sinful, making the child feel tainted and guilty. Brother Meagher's concern with "heroes and martyrs" of the past is linked to his salacious interest in violence. So insensitive is he that he takes Tom on a school outing whose purpose is to glorify Corny Dowley, the killer of Tom's father. Tom conceals his pain and confusion from his mother, but when he attempts to share with a sympathetic nun his bewilderment about sexuality and his fear that he is literally and figuratively untouchable in the townspeople's eyes, she, too, rejects him.

By the novel's end in the 1970s, most of the characters have died, old animosities have muted, and Tom has grown into a gentle, solitary man who remains bewildered by the confessions in Sarah's diary:

> Ever since he read in the diaries about the events that followed his father's death, Tom has been trying to comprehend them. Dowley found the excuse for his vengeance in the troubles there were, and that was natural enough. But the extraordinariness of what happened next bewilders Tom. There'd always been talk of the Rollestons' slaughtering their way to the island, but there'd been talk as well of how they'd been decent at the time of the Famine, and they'd been decent to his mother and they'd been decent to him. Funny the way a thing like the other would afflict them, the way they couldn't come to terms with it. (198)

Tom, whose ability to forgive is almost saintly, is now the master of a dilapidated Big House on an island of the dead, for Carriglas has been a cemetery since ancient times. He knows that he and Patty will remain there, unmarried; he knows that he will never attempt to retrieve a sliver of Carriglas' former glory by transforming it into a hotel. With the deaths of Patty and Tom, Fogarty's dream of dissolution will be realised.

In the short story "Timothy's Birthday" (discussed in an earlier chapter), the decline of a Big House in contemporary Ireland is poignant not because of any nostalgia for a lost tradition but rather because of the familial alienation that underlies it. Odo, whose medieval name bespeaks his inability to accept the changing mores of the present, alienates his only child and therefore heir to the estate, however derelict, because Timothy's homosexuality repels him. Timothy's hurt manifests itself in the petty cruelty of sending his street hustler lover to take his place at the birthday celebration lovingly prepared by his parents, and they must face the mournful reality that Timothy prefers Dublin life to the decaying house of his parents. Trevor does not imply that the decline of the estate can really be reversed or even that it should be mourned. The real source of regret is the impasse between father and son, and a wife/mother's sad recognition that the breach is irreparable.

Similarly, in Trevor's most recent novel, *The Story of Lucy Gault* (discussed in the final chapter), which traces a Big House family's decline and fall from the 1920s to the present, the dying out of the line, the anticipated metamorphosis of the house into a school or a hotel, is viewed with equanimity by Lucy, the sole surviving family member. Regrets abound in the novel, not for the passing of an era, but rather for missed opportunities, unvoiced emotions, and the sometimes bitter vicissitudes of daily life.

William Trevor, as a "lace curtain" Irish Protestant, brings a unique perspective to his Big House fiction. Although he uses such recognisable conventions of Big House literature as the alignment of the decaying estate with the declining class that inhabits it and the "genealogical breakdown" of the Ascendancy family (Kreilkamp, 1998: 22), he often eschews the familiarity of convention, compels the reader to examine characters on their own terms, not as familiar types. His landowners are by turn arrogant, benevolent and misguided, rather than calculatedly cruel or rapacious. Ignorance rather than viciousness underlies their errors.

Trevor resists adherence to convention not because he wishes to be an apologist for the Ascendancy, but rather because as an author he consistently avoids typecasting human beings. In addition, Trevor's Big House fiction explores his lifelong concern with power and its abuses. Unequal marriages, vulnerable children, the economically disadvantaged, the voiceless — all are frequent denizens of the "other people's worlds" that Trevor creates. In his Big House fiction, dispossession and the assumption of entitlement breed a sick society, a pathology he dissects most completely in "The News from Ireland". The Pulvertafts are not monsters, but they cocoon themselves in reassuring myths that enable them to "learn to live with things", wilfully ignorant about their complicity in the Famine's catastrophe.

Not surprisingly, then, he fulfils Fogarty's wish that the estate decay "back into the clay" when he writes *The Silence in the Garden*. The Big House cannot be rehabilitated; it can make way for the future. And although the Catholic populace that displaces the Rollestons, a displacement symbolised by the Cornelius Dowley Bridge, are no more angels of light than were the Big House family, and although Timothy saddens his parents by his refusal to return home and reclaim the decaying ancestral home, both are forward-looking, seeking a future rather than exhuming a decayed past. Lucy Gault, who has immured herself like a museum piece, achieves a certain peace in the end by reconciling herself to the past. But it is entirely appropriate that at the end of the novel she anticipates both the sale of the Big House after her death and the eroding power of the Catholic Church, placing herself in a continuum of inevitable change.

Chapter Five

"Poor Protestants"

Despite Trevor's chameleon-like ability to take on the coloration of people far removed from his own experience — though a man, he writes empathetically about women; though an expatriate for many years, he still writes so convincingly about Ireland that poet Eamon Grennan once commented in a conversation, "He picks up a stone and turns it over, and he knows the place" — he is a self-described "small-town Irish Protestant" (Stout, 1989–90: 131), a fact that is easy to forget simply because Trevor moves so deftly among his Catholic characters. As Robert Tracy has noted, Trevor belongs to the Protestant middle class that produced Yeats, Beckett and Synge, a class that "lived and worked among the Catholic majority and so were more readily exposed to the antithetical narratives that have traditionally shaped Irish Catholic and Protestant identities . . ." (1985: 296).

Growing up as he did in a newly independent Irish state, Trevor witnessed the decline of his echelon of Irish society. "Poor Protestants in Ireland are a sliver of people caught between the past — Georgian Ireland with its great houses and all the rest of it — and the new, bustling, Catholic state" (Stout, 1989–90: 131). In the same interview, Trevor credits this very marginality as lending clarity to his view of the world.

In *Reading Turgenev* (1991) and "Lost Ground" (1992), that familiar world is rendered into cautionary tales of characters unwilling to extricate themselves from the past and take their place in Ireland's ongoing history. The price of this intransigence is extinction. In a recent story, "Of the Cloth", a Church of Ireland pastor who has seen his world dwindle offers companionship to a Catholic curate bewildered by the erosion of his own cherished certainties. The two men transcend their religious differences and recognise their common humanity, their shared Irishness and, uncomfortably, their marginality as clergymen in an increasingly secularised Ireland.

In his memoir, *Excursions in the Real World*, Trevor declares that "I was born into a minority that all my life has seemed in danger of withering away" (*ERW, xiii*):

> The insult and repression that for centuries had been the response to Irish aspirations, the murders perpetrated by the Black and Tans, the heartbreak of the Civil War, were all to be expunged in de Valera's dream of a land "bright with cosy homesteads . . ."

> But dreams remain dreams unless practical steps are taken: some body of good men would have to ensure that all the people of Ireland lived the life "that God desire men should live". Quite naturally, de Valera turned to his priests, and quite naturally Protestants felt uneasy. (*xiii*)

Trevor recalls the dilapidated Big Houses filling up with "shopkeepers and clerks and poor relations"; Mrs Orpen, who may have been the model for Miss Middleton in "The Distant Past", standing when the radio broadcast "God Save the King" (and causing Trevor and his siblings to giggle when they were children); and how "Keeping faith with the irretrievable past — no matter how comic a form it took — was often the hallmark of the dispossessed" (*xiv*). As a youth, he imagined a future similar to that of so many of his fictional characters: "serving in a grocer's shop or a draper's, or as a bank clerk" (*xv*).

Canon Moran in "August Saturday", the eponymous Attracta, and the Famine-era Fogarty of "The News from Ireland" are among the characters drawn from Trevor's own background. In "Lost Ground" and *Reading Turgenev* (half of a pair of novellas published as *Two Lives*), Trevor plumbs this world of middle-class Protestant Ireland, North and South, revealing his increasing concern with his country's history. The characters in both works are faced with the choice of clinging to an obsolete or even vicious past or reconciling themselves with their Catholic neighbours; their failure to do so has tragic consequences.

The central characters of *Reading Turgenev*, the Dallons and the Quarrys, are Protestant families living in the midlands, where, because his father's job required frequent moves, Trevor spent an itinerant childhood. The novel has a dual time setting — 1950s and 1980s Ireland. In the 1950s, the Protestants in the townland of Culleen are a dwindling lot, as is evidenced by the scanty congregation at their Sunday services. The Quarrys — Elmer and his sisters, Rose and Matilda — continue to run the drapery shop that has been in the family for over a century, yet they recognise that changing times are rendering the business obsolete: as the sisters reflect, ". . . already Quarry's was a relic from another age. If the line came to an end the business would pass to distant cousins in Athy, who would probably sell it" (*TL*, 7). Their surname suggests their situation: theirs is a nearly exhausted quarry.

Elmer Quarry is unwilling to abandon hope, and proceeds to follow the patrilineal custom of marrying a younger wife to continue the family line. But times have changed, and Elmer has not fully realised that "All over the country wealth had passed into the hands of a new Catholic middle class, changing the nature of provincial life as it did so" (5). So he begins a passionless courtship of Mary Louise Dallon, one of the townland's few marriageable Protestant women.

The Dallons are likewise a family in decline, as is evidenced by the increasing dilapidation of their "modest" farmhouse. Mr and Mrs Dallon struggle to keep their unsteady son, James, interested in the family farm, for, like their neighbours, they fear the alternative:

> At that time, from the town and from the land around it, young men were making their way to England or America. . . . Families everywhere were affected by emigration, and the Protestant fraction of the population increasingly looked as if it would never recover. There was no fat on the bones of this shrinking community; there were no reserves of strength. Its very life was eroded by the bleak economy of the times. (14)

Mary Louise marries Elmer not because she loves him but because she desires a change from the dreary routine of farm life, having never set her ambitions higher than the prospect of working in a local shop.

The marriage is from the outset disastrous: though he secretly entertains sexual fantasies about some of the town's Catholic women — perhaps rendered exotic by their difference — Elmer is shocked to discover that in marital relations he is impotent; his shame manifests itself in alcoholism. Mary Louise, assumed by the townspeople to be the reason for the couple's childlessness, must endure not only a loveless, sexless marriage but also the unrelenting criticism of Elmer's unmarried sisters, who bitterly resent their brother's marriage.

Mary Louise escapes her unhappy life through a rekindled interest in her frail cousin, Robert, her childhood love. Robert, a sensitive, romantic young man, is likewise part of a dying Protestant breed — literally so. Unable to have an independent life because of his poor health, he lives with his mother, spending his days re-creating First World War battles with his toy soldiers and reading the novels of Turgenev. Though the relationship is unconsummated, Mary Louise learns for the first time what a tragic mistake her marriage has been, for Robert kindles her dormant passion. Ironically, she realises her passionate feelings only after his untimely death.

Sexual incapacity and childlessness, then, accelerate the decline of this Protestant community: Mary Louise and Elmer remain childless, Elmer's sisters never marry, Robert dies prematurely. Only Mary Louise's sister, Letty, breaks this cycle of decline, and she does so by marrying a Catholic.

Letty's relationship with the Catholic veterinarian Dennehy marks a turning point in the Protestant community, for though her parents secretly oppose the match, Trevor makes it clear that only through such unions will the Protestant community survive. Letty will not share her sister's sexual shock and disappointment, for she and Dennehy consummate their relationship before marriage — and Trevor's language is significant: "He took liberties she had not permitted Gargan or Billie Lyndon to take. In time she laid her head against the car seat and gave herself to them" (91). Symbolically, Letty's willing sexual acquiescence to Dennehy reflects a changing relationship between Irish Protestant and Irish Catholic. But Trevor does not merely align sex and power here, placing the Catholic male in the dominant role once occupied by the English and Anglo-Irish: he carefully avoids the distasteful and too-common literary practice of fetishising the woman's body, sexualising the "other". Letty is neither an exotic colleen nor the spoils of the struggle. She freely chooses Dennehy, and their union is auspicious.

And in fact, the wedding marks a new, fragile alliance between Protestant and Catholic communities. The fact that the reception takes place at the Dennehy family pub and that one of the wedding gifts is a picture of the Virgin and the

Sacred Heart secretly offends Mrs Dallon, but she and her husband publicly express joy about the marriage. Trevor describes the wedding reception with wry humour: catching sight of a vigil-lighted religious picture in the Dennehy home, "All of a sudden Mrs Dallon found herself wondering whom [her son] would marry" (156). But though the alcohol-befuddled Elmer questions the match — ". . . poor Protestants for donkey's years, why would they be pleased to see their grandchildren brought up holy Romans?" (146) — Trevor makes it clear that this is an auspicious event, for the Dennehys' marriage is not only happy, but fertile: Letty is soon pregnant.

The Dennehys are likewise distinctive in the Protestant community for their attitude toward the past. Their rehabilitation of an abandoned farmhouse into a thriving home is a marked contrast to Elmer's misguided attempts to continue a declining family business and Robert's pathetic attempts to re-enact past battles with his toy soldiers. Even Robert's romantic trysts with Mary Louise take place in an overgrown graveyard.

But Mary Louise herself manifests the most disturbing inability to face the future. After Robert's death, she invents a fantasy life to assuage the very real misery of her marriage. She furnishes an attic room with Robert's possessions and there indulges in an imaginary marriage with her dead cousin. So happy does this invented life make her that she feigns more madness than she suffers just to be committed to an institution, where she can escape Elmer's seedy decline and his sisters' petty malice. She succeeds in this quest for thirty-one years, until the unthinkable happens: the institution closes, and a now-elderly Elmer arrives to take her home.

With age, in 1980s Ireland, Elmer acquires a new dignity. After decades of passivity in the face of his sisters' bullying, he asserts his loyalty to his wife and his determination to bring her home. Mary Louise's only wish, which Elmer grants, is that she eventually be buried beside her cousin.

Three decades have solidified the decline of the Protestant community, a decline that was already apparent in the 1950s. The older Dallons have died, and their dream of keeping the farm in the family has withered: their son James discovers that his sons have no interest in the land. Elmer finally acquiesces to the fact that times have changed, and sells the family business. Only Letty and Dennehy thrive.

Reading Turgenev reflects some of Trevor's personal reality: unemployment drove him to reluctant emigration in the 1950s. As he once observed in an interview: "I hated leaving Ireland. I was very bitter at the time"; but significantly, he added, "But, had it not happened, I think I might never have written at all" (Bruckner, 1990: C14).

What Trevor has created in *Reading Turgenev* is no mere reminiscence of the world of his youth; instead, he once again draws on his training as a historian to create a symbolic reading of Ireland's past. The world of the Dallons and the Quarrys is a microcosm of post-Second World War Ireland, and their pervasive inability to shake themselves loose from the past and align themselves with the future mirrors the plight of Protestants displaced by the political and economic changes wrought by independence.

Trevor seems less interested in arguing the unfairness of the early nation's tendency to equate Irishness with Catholicism than he is with urging the abandonment of a way of life that has become obsolete, of a self-definition that has been rendered irrelevant. In that sense, his "poor Protestant" fiction is not so different from his writings about the Troubles, for in both cases repetition of the past can be lethal.

In "Lost Ground", Trevor offers one of his rare forays into Northern Ireland to illustrate the dangers of clinging to the myths of the past. The protagonists of the story, the Leeson family, are middle-class Protestant farmers, but the world they inhabit is in some regards less a mirror image of Trevor's other Protestant lives than a journey through the looking-glass. Although in most of Trevor's fiction about middle-class Protestants his characters belong to the Church of Ireland, the Leesons seem to be Ulster Presbyterians. The power structure in Northern Ireland is quite different here, for the Leesons are in the majority, their Catholic neighbours an embattled minority; the world they inhabit is not the emergent Catholic state of *Reading Turgenev* but rather the fiercely contested Six Counties that remained part of Britain when Ireland was partitioned. Whereas in *Reading Turgenev* religious differences are often manifested humorously, in "Lost Ground" Trevor reveals the ugly face of religious bigotry.

"Lost Ground" appeared in *The New Yorker* in 1992 but remained uncollected until the 1996 *After Rain*. Its central characters, the Leesons, have been actively engaged in the suppression of Catholics, and their thuggish son, Garfield, who, ironically, works as a "butcher's assistant", derives his greatest satisfaction from being a "'hard-man volunteer'" who delights in boasting about killing Catholics. Every July, the Leesons volunteer their lands for the Orange march commemorating King William's victory at the Battle of the Boyne, while their Catholic neighbours stay indoors fearfully. The Leesons' political beliefs have caused a deep rift in the family, for though they express sorrow over their estrangement from their daughter Hazel, they have had a hand in causing it:

> The tit-for-tat murders spawned by that same hard-man mentality, the endless celebration of a glorious past on one side and the picking over of ancient rights on the other, the reluctance to forgive — all this was what Hazel had run away from. (*AR*, 155)

In an incident recalling Trevor's earlier "ghost" stories ("The Raising of Elvira Tremlett", "The Death of Peggy Morrissey" — or Peggy Meehan, as it is named in the *Collected Stories*), the Leesons' teenaged son, the tellingly named Milton, encounters a mysterious woman who, he is convinced, "'wasn't alive'". Asserting that she is "St Rosa", the woman kisses Milton — a "'holy'" kiss, she calls it — and urges him, "'Don't be afraid when the moment comes. . . . There is too much fear'" (153).

St Rosa is a decidedly ordinary apparition. Milton notes her frail slenderness, her black hair, her dark coat "which did not seem entirely clean" (148), and the scarf at her throat. There is nothing exotic in her appearance, and at first Milton speculates that she may be stealing apples from his father's orchard.

Milton comes to believe that the woman is St Rose of Viterbo, about whom he knows nothing except her name, mentioned to him by a Catholic priest. According to Butler's *Lives of the Saints*, Rose was a thirteenth-century child preacher who urged her compatriots to resist Emperor Frederick II's occupation of their city in his campaign to conquer the Papal states. Rose's preaching endangered her life and resulted in her family's banishment. Only after Frederick's death, which Rose had foretold, was she able to return to Viterbo (1985, 275–6). Rose was beleaguered by both secular and religious authorities. Refused admittance to a convent because she could not afford a dowry, she was thwarted by Pope Innocent IV in her attempts to live in a self-founded religious community. Having returned to her parents, she died when she was approximately 17 (1985, 276).

St Rosa is thus an appropriate name for Milton's mysterious woman, for he, too, lives in an embattled country; he, too, becomes a controversial young preacher; he, too, suffers at the hands of both secular and religious leaders. Trevor is careful to leave ambiguous the actual nature of Milton's visitor. She is older than the historical Rose was at the time of her death; she wears modern dress; she speaks English.

As in the earlier stories, whether this woman is visitation, reality, or figment of Milton's imagination, she has a profound psychological impact on the boy's life. Haunted by her words, Milton unsuccessfully seeks advice, first from his dour brother-in-law, the Reverend Herbert Cutcheon, who chalks the event up to adolescent hormones, then urges the boy to keep silent. Milton then horrifies his family by confiding in a Catholic priest, but sees that Father Mulhall is struggling to contain his anger. The priest has heard of Garfield's vicious reputation, rankles at the implicit threat of the annual Orange Parade, and, in a touch of Trevor's wry humour, wonders what business Catholic saints have appearing to Protestant boys.

Milton, like the Puritan poet his name recalls, feels compelled to justify the ways of God to men and women. Inhabiting his own "paradise lost", a lovely landscape corrupted by bigotry and violence, and experiencing, as John Milton did, the ugly face of civil conflict, this latter-day Milton cycles to neighbouring villages to preach St Rosa's message of forgiveness:

> St Rosa could forgive the brutish soldiers and their masked adversaries, one or another of them responsible for each of the shattered motorcars and shrouded bodies that came and went on the television screen. (172)

He speaks of Hazel's estrangement, the Orange Parade, and Fr Mulhall's anger. Milton's message of peace and forgiveness contrasts ironically to the sermons of another preacher in the family, his great-uncle Willie, who, before his age prevented it, used to expound his anti-Catholic bigotry:

> Sometimes he spoke of what happened in Rome,
> facts he knew to be true: how the Pope drank him-
> self into a stupor and had to have the sheets of his
> bed changed twice in a night, how the Pope's own
> mother was among the women who came and went
> in the papal ante-rooms. (164)

Though these words seem absurd, the rantings of a fanatic, they have a threatening underside, for Uncle Willie also "laid down that a form of cleansing was called for, that vileness could be exorcised by withering it out of existence" (164).

Like those earlier figures whom Kristin Morrison chris-tens "holy fools" — such as Cynthia of "Beyond the Pale" or the title character of "Attracta" — all of whom call for for-giveness and reconciliation, Milton preaches an unwelcome message. But unlike these women, whose punishment was to be ignored, Milton's story has a more sinister ending. Em-barrassed by their son's notoriety, the Leesons put him un-der close surveillance; he eats his meals in solitude and is often locked in his room. Eventually he is murdered by two men, one of them his own brother, Garfield. And though there is talk of the Provisional IRA in the neighbourhood, Hazel, who returns home for the funeral, studies the faces at the graveside and realises the shocking truth: "All of them knew." Disturbingly, Garfield's "hard-man reputation had been threatened, and then enhanced" (182) by the murder of his brother.

The Leesons' desperate attempts to salvage their reputa-tion result in a decidedly Pyrrhic victory. Their farm, which has been in the family since 1809, will become "lost ground": of their remaining children, Hazel is estranged from her fam-ily and her country, Stewart has Down's Syndrome, and Garfield has in the past declared his intention to sell the land should he inherit it. Noting the multiple puns of the story's title, Morrison concludes:

> The final and greatest lost ground is peace itself: in-
> stead of making progress toward recognising their
> brotherhood and learning to live together, this
> community has lost ground by fostering and condon-
> ing fratricide. (1991, 167)

The Leesons — and their name itself is a pun — fail to learn
the lessons of the past, and in their failure to escape their
history, they must live with its nightmares.

Trevor's Irish fiction frequently grapples with the meaning of the past: his explorations of Irish sectarian violence
assert urgently that the past must not repeat itself; his studies of Irish family life frequently reveal melancholy souls
trapped by their own personal histories and relentless
memories. Never sentimental about the past, Trevor insists
instead on its crippling emotional power.

In *Reading Turgenev* and "Lost Ground", as in Trevor's earlier fiction, characters' inability to free themselves from the
past renders their lives sterile, both literally and figuratively.
But in earlier works, the power of the past seems more inexorable, individuals' choices more circumscribed. We never
expect the title character of "Attracta" to succeed in her
saintly mission of ending the violence in Northern Ireland; the
butler Fogarty's wish to stem the cycle of invasion and oppression that is Irish history ("The News from Ireland") is not one
that he will ever see realised. For these Protestant characters,
history is comparable to Stephen Dedalus's nightmare.

Reading Turgenev and "Lost Ground", despite their melancholy tone, are not quite so fatalistic. Letty Dallon Dennehy
refuses to share the plight of her dying Protestant community.
As the heartbroken and guilt-ridden Leesons stand at Milton's
grave, their daughter Hazel thinks:

> The family would not ever talk about the day, but
> through their pain they would tell themselves that

> Milton's death was the way things were, the way things
> had to be. That was their single consolation. (183)

But the Leesons do not *have* to accept Garfield's brutality;
they do not *have* to cling to the traditions of the past.

These Protestant cautionary tales offer a more guardedly
optimistic view of Ireland's history. Trevor plumbs the world
of his own middle-class Protestant background, and the moral
of his stories is that those who lock their identity in a vanishing past are doomed to exclusion from Ireland's future.

In "Of the Cloth", first published in 1998, Trevor explores not the displacement of the middle-class Protestant
Ireland of his youth but rather the erosion of Catholic
hegemony in contemporary Ireland. This poignant, gently
ironic story unites an elderly Church of Ireland rector who
has witnessed the vanishing of his familiar world and a young
Catholic priest glimpsing the frightening possibility that his
old certainties are crumbling.

Rev. Grattan Fitzmaurice's name is a nugget of Irish history: his surname recalls his Norman antecedents; his given
name his parents' tribute to Henry Grattan, the eighteenth-
century parliamentary leader who championed increased
political rights for Ireland, including Catholic emancipation,
despite his own Anglo-Irish background. Elderly, unmarried,
and ministering to a dwindling flock, Rev. Fitzmaurice notes,
without ill feeling, that the local Catholic church is thriving,
and believes he sees in Fr MacPartlan's "ruddy features" and
Fr Leahy's "untroubled smile" evidence of "the simplicity of
total belief, of belonging and being in touch" (*HB*, 24). Fitzmaurice's isolation is heightened by his belief that he is "out
of touch" with contemporary life, and recalls his father's
melancholy pronouncement, when 40 years earlier he observed the fading away of the Church of Ireland community,
that "'We are a remnant'" (23).

"Of the Cloth" presents an Ireland in which Fogarty (from "The News from Ireland") might see his dream fulfilled: Big Houses have "fallen back to the clay" (22), the very words Fogarty used to described his hopes for the Pulvertaft estate. In the years following independence and partition, Rev. Fitzmaurice's people have been elbowed out of the way: "Risen from near-suppression, the great Church of Rome inherited all Ireland" (23–4). In the process, Irish Protestants' contributions to Irish history stand in sad contrast to a now-"withering" (Fogarty's word again) Church of Ireland:

> It was an irony that they should be [a remnant], for it had been Protestant leaders in the past — Wolfe Tone and Thomas Davis, Emmet and Parnell, the Henry Grattan after whom Grattan was named — who had in their different times been the inspiration for the Catholic Ireland that had come about, and Grattan knew that its birth was Ireland's destiny and her due. (23)

Contemporary commentators on Irish identity, most notably Edna Longley and John Wilson Foster, have more pointedly argued that the plurality of Ireland must not be ignored, particularly that devaluing the contribution of such Protestant political figures listed above to the emergence of the Irish nation not only does history a disservice but also impedes the formation of a viable solution to Northern Ireland's fragmentation.

Although "Of the Cloth" echoes "The News from Ireland", it also subverts Fogarty and his apocalyptic vision of Ireland. In contrast to Erskine, the bigoted, harsh, one-armed Protestant estate-manager in "News" is Con Tonan, a Catholic farmer disabled by the loss of an arm who worked as Rev. Fitzmaurice's gardener for 28 years. Erskine is an ominous figure, a man who dislikes the Irish and feels neither sympathetic nor indulgent toward the starving workers under his command. By marrying the once-compassionate governess, Anna Maria Heddoe, he will symbolically sever any possibility of connection between the Big House and its Catholic tenants.

Con Tonan, in contrast, inadvertently forges a fragile link between Catholic and Protestant in his community. Fitzmaurice's kindness in hiring the disabled Tonan and training him to tend the rectory garden has not gone unnoticed, and the old man is startled and touched when Tonan's widow reveals to him how much her husband loved going to Ennismolach Rectory: the experience gave Con not only balm for his injured self-respect but also the mutual friendship of Grattan Fitzmaurice, a man whom he would otherwise never have gotten to know because of the religious divide that separated them.

In current debates about Ireland's future, and particularly discussions of what relationship will develop between Northern Ireland and the Republic of Ireland, much has been written about the meanings of "Ireland" and "Irishness". Declan Kiberd, Shaun Richards, David Cairns and many others have discussed the "construction" and "invention" of Ireland; the founders of Field Day envisioned a "Fifth Province" of the imagination, a neutral ground whereon new definitions of cultural identity might be forged and sectarian divides bridged. Edna Longley's and John Wilson Foster's discussions of Protestant identity argue that what passes for unity is often Catholic Nationalism in disguise, and contend that Ireland's plurality must be acknowledged, a plurality that recognises difference rather than trying to pretend that some sort of Irish melting-pot is possible.

"Of the Cloth" subtly embodies much of this heady, crucial debate. With exquisite sensitivity, Trevor depicts what may be the beginning of a "beautiful friendship" (to quote *Casablanca*) between Rev. Fitzmaurice and Fr Leahy, the young curate at Con Tonan's church. Despite their proximity, despite their civility toward one another, Catholics and Protestants in this rural area live in self-imposed segregation, and neither priest has ever visited Fitzmaurice's rectory before. When Fr Leahy unexpectedly drops in after Con's funeral, Fitzmaurice wrongly assumes that the younger man has been instructed by Fr MacPartlan to do so, an act of charity to the elderly man. Noticing on his table a copy of *The Irish Times* detailing the notorious case of Fr Brendan Smyth, the Norbertine priest convicted on numerous counts of sexual abuse of children, Rev. Fitzmaurice turns the paper face down, not wanting to cause pain to his visitor. As the two men talk, their common experience becomes apparent: Fitzmaurice remembers how the child Leahy had waved to his passing car when the boy sat with his brothers on the whitewashed wall of their farm, and the two men discuss family and neighbours.

Yet Fitzmaurice gradually realises that what he thought was an act of charity on the young priest's part is far more complicated. Fr Leahy, grown tentatively confidential in the encroaching darkness, hints to Rev. Fitzmaurice his own bewilderment at a changing society, a church whose power, once assured, is slipping. As Fitzmaurice muses:

> He often read in the paper these days that in the towns Mass was not as well attended as it had been even a few years ago. In the towns marriage was not always bothered with, confession and absolution passed by. A different culture, they called it, in which restraint and prayer were not the way, as once they had been. . . . In the different culture Christ's imitation offered too little. (36)

The young priest confides that Fr MacPartlan comes to breakfast with tear-reddened eyes, and hints at his own loneliness: "'I never left Ireland,' Father Leahy said. 'I never been [sic]outside it'" (37); neither has Grattan. Fitzmaurice comes to realise that he and the priests, three "men of the cloth", have far more in common than he had previously assumed. Fr Leahy's visit was not in fact an act of charity toward an old man, but instead provoked by the young priest's need to be touched by the sort of kindness that Fitzmaurice had extended to Con Tonan: for Fr MacPartlan had said, "'you'd given Con Tonan his life back. Even though Con Tonan wasn't one of your own'" (38). In fact, Fitzmaurice does attempt to comfort the younger man: "'You're not left bereft, you know'" (38).

Fr Leahy's visit stirs Rev. Fitzmaurice's sympathetic imagination, and he empathises with both priests' frightening realisations that their world is eroding, for he has experienced a similar loss. Yet he also recognises their common Irishness, an Irishness that is differently defined: Fitzmaurice thinks of history, of people who have suffered greatly but have refused to submit, and it is clear that he regards them as his people, himself as an Irishman. He thinks with affection of the beautiful rural scenes he loves: "The sound, the look, the shape of Ireland, and Ireland's rain and Ireland's sunshine, and Ireland's living and Ireland's dead: all that" (37). He imagines the young priest's different but no less loved version of Ireland: watching football matches and sharing a post-game pint in the local pub; "the memory of the cars going by, his bare feet on the cobbles of the yard, the sacrifice he had made, and his faithful coming to him, the cross emblazoned on a holy robe. Good Catholic Ireland, a golden age" (37).

This delicately drawn encounter offers solace for both men in their different lonelinesses, and Rev. Fitzmaurice concludes, "Small gestures mattered now . . ." (39). Indeed, this is a story filled with small gestures of hope and endurance. After Con's death, Fitzmaurice's Protestant housekeeper describes him as a "decent" man, a compliment that in the past was often reserved for Protestants. "Protestants were often called decent. You knew where you were with Protestants: that was said often in those days" (32). Con's widow warms the minister's heart with her gratitude for his kindness. Two communities kept at a distance by history and habit have become a little less estranged.

William Trevor has long recognised the complexities of Irish identity, and has written "inside the skin" of diverse Irish characters. He never downplays the cruelties of the past, the inequities wrought by abused power. Yet in his fiction, his most eloquent arguments against repeating history's trage-dies have been his depictions of lives shattered and thwarted by revenge, by bitter memories that strangle the living.

Trevor's "poor Protestant" fiction bespeaks its author's comprehension of Ireland's religious/cultural divides and the mutual misunderstanding that perpetuates them. Having long recognised that Ireland's house has many mansions, Trevor understands that, to quote Hugh O'Donnell, the schoolmas-ter in Brian Friel's *Translations*, ". . . it is not the literal past, the 'facts' of history, that shape us, but images of the past embodied in language", and that "we must never cease re-newing those images; because once we do, we fossilise" (Friel, 1984: 445). Embracing Catholic and Protestant alike, Trevor's fiction urges the imaginative thinking that that re-newal entails.

Chapter Six

De-Colleenising Ireland

Throughout his career, William Trevor has written sympathetically of women who, despite their varied national and
economic backgrounds, suffer the injustice of living in male-
dominated societies. Women's names provide the titles for
several of his novels and many of his short stories; women
characters function as the central intelligence in many other
works.

In Trevor's Irish fiction, women are frequently rendered
powerless by economic exigency, family expectation, and
religious pressure. Despite the poignancy of these women's
constrained lives, Trevor does not suggest that Irish women
alone suffer from limited opportunities. Trevor's Irish males
likewise find themselves as James Baldwin once wrote of
Black American men: "their heads bumped abruptly against
the low ceiling of their actual possibilities" (1965, 104). Nor
does one find in Trevor the monstrous males of Edna
O'Brien's rural fiction: in "The Ballroom of Romance", for
instance, Bridie's father is neither violent nor abusive, but
instead pathetically aware of how his own physical disability
and the death of his wife have rendered him dependent on
his daughter and prevented her from escaping a dreary life.

Though Trevor has continued to write sympathetically of
thwarted lives of both genders, in the 1990 collection *Family*

Sins he embarks on an assault against stereotypes of Irish women, reductive images employed by both English colonisers and Irish colonised, but profoundly at odds with the lives of real Irish women.

The identification of Ireland with female icons — Hibernia, Erin, the old woman, Dark Rosaleen, the colleen — has for centuries been a potent and pernicious tendency. The origin of this identification of woman and nation remains under debate, with some scholars contending that it is rooted in early Celtic culture, whereas others assert that it was a result of colonisation (Innes, 1993: 26). Curiously, these stereotypes historically have been embraced by Irish and English alike: the metaphor of Ireland as oppressed woman both in the guises of helpless maiden and dispossessed mother appears in many Irish literary manifestations, including the *aisling* poems; woman as militant standard-bearer fuelled Irish nationalist posters and political cartoons. Conversely, English political cartoonists juxtaposed the image of weeping, pliant Hibernia with a simian-appearing male revolutionary of the Fenian movement to indicate to English Victorian audiences the difference between good (i.e. tractable) Irish and bad (i.e. rebellious) ones (Curtis, 1971: 25, 37). As C.L. Innes observes, in the Victorian English consciousness a considerable distinction was drawn between the idealised concept of Ireland and the often-despised Irish people:

> . . . if Hibernia embodies the extreme of angelic femininity dreamed by Victorian Englishmen — beautiful, graceful, spiritualised and passive — Hibernians are her opposite — bestial, dirty, loutishly masculine, aggressive and ugly: the extreme of masculine bestiality feared by Victorian Englishmen, and in this aspect like representations of African and Indian men. (1993, 14)

As the diverse women in Anne Crilly's 1988 documentary *Mother Ireland* point out, whether the image be the poor old woman with her captive four green fields, the sorrowful Rosaleen awaiting rescue from foreign oppression, the defiant Hibernia urging rebellion, or the sweet colleen beckoning the romantic tourist, such reductive images are false and unfair, bearing little resemblance to real Irish women. As Lorna Reynolds has observed,

> . . . the women of my generation and of the preceding generation were more than able to hold their own in a man's world, and I cannot recall a single, simple colleen among them. . . . the women of Ireland, whether we look for them in legend, literature, or life, do not correspond to the stereotypes that have, so mysteriously, developed in the fertile imaginations of men. (1983, 25)

Contemporary Irish women writers and visual artists such as Eavan Boland, Anne Devlin, Julia O'Faolain, Nuala Ní Dhomhnaill, Rita Duffy, Alice Maher and many others have laboured to free Irish women of restrictive stereotypes and given eloquent expression to the female experience in Ireland. Boland has assailed the persistence of female stereotypes, noting the difficulties of trying to find a poetic voice in a tradition that made women the "objects of Irish poems" (1995, 126). Real women's lives were often lost sight of in Irish poetry written by men, in which

> women . . . were often passive, decorative, raised to emblematic status. This was especially true where the woman and the idea of the nation were mixed: where the nation became a woman and the woman took on a national posture. (134–5)

Commenting on the tenacity of these images, Boland once commented in an interview:

My objections to this are ethical. If you consistently simplify women by making them national icons in poetry or drama you silence a great deal of the actual women in that past, who intimately depend on us, as writers, not to simplify them in the present. (Wilson, 1990: 87)

Nuala Ní Dhomhnaill agrees that such iconography is pernicious:

. . . there is a psychotic splitting involved where, the more the image of woman comes to stand for abstract concepts like justice, liberty, or national sovereignty, the more real women are denigrated and consigned barefoot and pregnant to the kitchen. (1996, 16)

In *Family Sins*, Trevor not only offers complex and credible portraits of Irish women, he also explodes Ireland's long-cherished female icons by pointing up the disparity between real and mythological women, the failings of a society that simultaneously romanticises and abuses women.

As Kristin Morrison has pointed out in her review of *Family Sins* (1991, 20), the very title of "Kathleen's Field" carries strong emotional associations: one thinks of Cathleen ní Houlihan pleading for the rescue of her four green fields. Trevor's title functions ironically here, however: Kathleen Hagerty is doomed to an unhappy, victimised life primarily because her culture, for all its veneration of mythical women, undervalues real ones.

The story is set in 1948, a time when the dreams of an independent nation were settling into the realities of an economically struggling state, where women's hopes for equality had been dashed by a discriminatory constitution, censorship and sexual repression limited individual freedom, and the special status accorded to the Catholic Church seemed a real threat to the possibility for a pluralistic society. As Declan Kiberd asserts:

> . . . the new state . . . would deny the manly woman epitomised by Constance Markievicz and Maud Gonne, opting instead for de Valera's maidens at the rural crossroads, themselves a pastoral figment of the late-Victorian imagination. (1995, 182–3)

Women in 1940s Ireland were losing ground. Rural women faced the limited prospects of late marriage or emigration (Kiberd, 1995: 477) and "an accompanying ethic of sexual continence . . . rooted less in the puritanism of the Catholic Church than in the need to avoid further subdivision of family farms . . ." (477). Kiberd further notes the irony that, despite the "official ideology enshrined in de Valera's 1937 Constitution, of a society which constructed itself on the sacredness of family life", in fact "Rural Ireland was filled with broken families" (477). As we shall see, de Valera's apparent inability to discern the realities of Irish women's lives later incurred Trevor's pointed irony in *Felicia's Journey*.

"Kathleen's Field" depicts a woman trapped by poverty, religion and family loyalty. Kathleen Hagerty's father is already in debt but longs to buy another field that will ensure financial security for his family. His only collateral is Kathleen, whose services as a maid are exchanged for a loan of money. The bargain is at once monstrous and complex: Kathleen's wages will be applied to the debt, so she will have nothing to show for at least ten years of work. At the same time, she is all too aware of her family's plight: seven of the ten children have emigrated, leaving herself, her mentally disabled sister, and her brother Con, who without the additional field will be unable to marry and to support his sisters after their parents' deaths.

Kathleen's life as maid to the Shaughnessy family is miserable: not only is she homesick, she is bullied and ridiculed by Mrs Shaughnessy, ignored by the son, and worst of all, subjected to Mr Shaughnessy's unwelcome sexual advances. Her emotional turmoil is great: her Catholic upbringing has made her both acutely aware of sin and ashamed to talk about sexual matters, so she can neither tell her parents nor determine whether she is guilty of sin in tolerating Shaughnessy's sexual exhibitionism. Haunted by her loving father's gratitude to her and her mother's calm argument that she is fortunate to have such an employment opportunity, Kathleen ultimately keeps silent, even though her misery will last for years. To Shaughnessy's public teasing about her possibly marrying someday, she thinks sadly that her plain looks have attracted no one except her unpleasant employer: it does not seem that Kathleen will be accorded the escape of marriage, either.

Part of what makes "Kathleen's Field" such a horrifying story is that the Hagertys are inherently good people, but economic constraint and worry about the future render them capable of viewing the sacrifice of their daughter's life as a boon rather than a blight. The inherent sexual inequality of their world, exacerbated by their poverty, deems their son's inheritance to be more important than their daughter's freedom.

But "Kathleen's Field" is more than a sympathetic portrait of a powerless woman. The mythical associations conjured up by its title assume a deliberate irony here. No rescue is imminent for Kathleen Hagerty, and her plight is not the stuff of high tragedy but rather a chronicle of "quiet desperation". Kathleen is exploited by an employer who assumes that because she is female and economically dependent upon him, she is by rights his sexual victim. Likewise, the Hagertys assume that because she is female, she will sacrifice her own desires for her family's sake. And, as Morrison observes of the story's protagonist: "this girl is not a queen or a countess in a parable where one national group or class exploits another; her oppressors are themselves Irish" (1991, 20). Yet although Morrison's point about the disparity between the mythical and the real Kathleen is well-taken, Kathleen's plight is in fact linked to English imperialism. Her "oppressors" may indeed be Irish, but her situation is rooted in Ireland's colonial past. The family's obsession with holding on to the family farm, the desire for a more fertile field, the near-dissolution of the family because of emigration — these problems have their source in Ireland's colonial history.

Further, the social pretensions of the Shaughnessys have historical roots as well, for in the wake of independence, a rising middle class attempted to assert its importance; some enjoyed a new-found prosperity. The Shaughnessys seem a type of the *paudeens* so despised by Yeats, though Kathleen is a far cry from the poet's idealised "peasantry". Mrs Shaughnessy, a shopkeeper with delusions of gentility, looks down upon Kathleen, considering this "country girl" barely civilised; yet having a maid gives the Shaughnessys status in their town. She robs the younger woman of her identity by calling her "Kitty", the name of a former maid, and forcing her to wear her predecessor's ill-fitting uniform. And, considering the fact that Kathleen is one of a long line of Shaughnessy maids, one wonders whether Mrs Shaughnessy is indeed as oblivious to her husband's sexual abuse as she appears to be. Even more disturbing is the ambiguity of the Hagerty family's reaction to Kathleen's unhappiness. Torn between her father's pathetic gratitude and her mother's pragmatic insistence that the bargain with the Shaughnessys must be fulfilled, Kathleen does not specify why she is so unhappy in her job; but her family does not try very hard to find out the sources of her misery, as if they cannot bear to know, because knowledge will in all probability change nothing. By leaving this gap in the narrative, Trevor opens up the horrifying possibility that even were the Hagertys to know of their daughter's sexual abuse, their desperate need for the field would compel them to leave her in the Shaughnessys' employ.

A sad reversal of her mythical predecessor, Kathleen Hagerty embodies the evils wrought by Ireland's colonial past — not only the inequities wrought by land seizure and foreign occupation, but also the psychological damage done to the Irish by the English and by themselves: a damaged sense of self-worth, an adoption of English materialism, and the construction of national myths painfully at odds with the realities of Irish life.

Trevor does not limit his scrutiny of female Irish stereotypes to Ireland's past, however. In "Events at Drimaghleen", Trevor uses a contemporary setting to undermine the very roots of Irish female stereotypes. Not only are we left in no doubt about the injustice of such reductive images, we are given female characters who defy any easy definition.

Maureen McDowd, youngest daughter of a farming couple, falls in love with the ne'er-do-well son of a possessive widow. The McDowds deplore what they see as a hopeless entanglement for Maureen, and when their daughter is missing from home overnight they assume she has eloped with Lancy Butler, a belief that causes McDowd to refer to her as "'a little bitch'". But when the McDowds arrive at the Butler farm they discover an almost unimaginable horror: Maureen, Lancy and Mrs Butler dead of shotgun wounds. Police and community alike conclude that Mrs Butler, who "had been obsessively possessive, hiding from no one her determination that no other woman should ever take her son away from her" (*CS*, 1089), killed Maureen in jealous rage; her son "by accident or otherwise" then killed his mother and in despair ended his own life.

Though Maureen is dead at the story's beginning, through her parents' grief we are made acutely aware of how unnecessary, how wasteful her death was. But Trevor complicates this rural tragedy, for Maureen's bleak story goes beyond her death. The McDowds reluctantly agree to be interviewed by an unscrupulous journalist, trusting that she will be honest, and tempted by a much-needed payment of £3,000. To their dismay, the journalist transforms their daughter's tragedy into a lurid tabloid distortion. The journalist concludes that Maureen herself was the murderer, "a saint by nature and possessing a saint's fervour, [who] on that fatal evening made up for all the sins she had ever resisted" (1096). The terrible irony is that the McDowds have unwittingly destroyed their daughter's reputation, and because they have accepted payment, must now live with a guilt that makes them wretched.

Trevor invests the McDowds' tragedy with political implications, for Hetty Fortune, the appropriately named journalist, is English, and her story is coloured by anti-Irish bigotry. Trevor has elsewhere provided biting accounts of English prejudice; here he likewise exposes bigotry's insidiousness. At the journalist's hands, Maureen becomes a stereotypical pure Irish maiden of notable piety, a "saint" who erupts into violence when her love for Lancy Butler is thwarted. The McDowds, despite their affection for Maureen, are dismayed by Fortune's characterisation of her, and their recollections of their daughter evoke, instead of a pious colleen, a very real young woman whose family's reticence prevented them from knowing her intimately. Other stereotypes colour the newspaper story: the investigating policeman is rendered dim and inept, a bumbling "Mick"; the Drimaghleen community becomes threateningly self-protective. Fortune intimates that fear of reprisal prevented the Gardaí from uncovering the truth: "*The Irish do not easily forgive the purloining of their latter-day saints*" (1097).

Through the collusion between her parents and Hetty Fortune, Maureen McDowd is "colleenised" into an unreal, reductive image. We bridle at the injustice of this process even as we pity the bereaved McDowds.

Robert Rhodes has pointed out that, in "Events at Dri-maghleen", Trevor deliberately withholds information: ultimately, no one will ever know the truth. Though forensic tests could probably have eliminated some of the confusion surrounding the crime, apparently no tests were performed — are the Gardaí at fault, as Fortune suggests? Furthermore, Trevor is silent about such telling details as the exact placement of the bodies at the crime scene and the locations of the wounds — details that would surely rule out one set of conclusions about possible culprits (1989, 45–8).

Just as Trevor leaves us bewildered about the identity of the murderer or murderers at Drimaghleen, he leaves us wondering about the real characters of the dead, particularly about Mrs Butler and Maureen McDowd, women whom others too readily explain away by stereotypes. Mrs Butler is characterised by her neighbours as the possessive, overprotective mother of an only son, but this too is a familiar stereotype of Irish women, too easy a dismissal of a life. We are told that Mrs Butler had miscarried frequently before giving birth to Lancy, that she was widowed when the child was only two, that their farm is located in an isolated spot. These bald statements both tease and trouble us, for they bespeak a life of pain and loneliness, a life that in death becomes grossly oversimplified. Immediately thereafter, we are made privy to Garda O'Kelly's speculations about rumours that ". . . Mrs Butler had been reputed to be strange in the head and given to furious jealousies where Lancy was concerned." He concludes, "In the kind of rage that people who'd known her were familiar with she had shot her son's sweetheart rather than suffer the theft of him" (1089).

The problem is, of course, that O'Kelly draws his conclusions from rumours, not facts. Because the possessive Irish mother is a familiar stereotype, it takes little to convince the Garda that he has reached a viable solution to the crime. Concerned as he is with the shock and suffering the

killings have caused in the community, he looks no further
for an explanation. On the other hand, accepting the rumours necessitates putting paid to another image of Irish
women, the nurturing "Mother Ireland". The community's
version of a wrathful, shotgun-toting Mrs Butler, stunting her
son's emotional and sexual growth, becomes difficult to sen-
timentalise. Ultimately, whether one accepts the official version of the deaths or searches for a different explanation,
Trevor forces his reader to confront and reassess reductive
images of Irish women.

The mythologising of Maureen McDowd is likewise disturbing. Hetty Fortune's characterisation of Maureen, unlike
her description of Mrs Butler, apparently has little foundation in reality, but her English readers, familiar with the
stereotype of the colleen, have little difficulty transferring it
to a real woman. But Trevor has raised too many questions
in our minds for us to be capable of accepting this characterisation.

In this deliberate ambiguity, Trevor deals a subtle yet
critical blow to the stereotyping of Irish women. The events
at Drimaghleen disturb us, rouse our perennial human hunger for the security of certainty. But certainty is precisely
what Trevor withholds here: in fact, he discredits the misguided desire for certainty that finds stereotyping a comfortable means of explaining away troubling complexities in
human behaviour.

In "August Saturday", Trevor dissects not an Irish female
stereotype but rather one of the most enduring women of
Irish myth: Grainne. Certainly, both Grainne and Deirdre,
whose stories of flight from sexual domination end in
doomed love affairs, have inspired varied literary treatments.
But Deirdre is more often portrayed as a victim, a sorrowful, abused woman whose despair after her lover Naoise's
death results in suicide. Grainne is a more problematic character, for according to myth, after her lover Diarmaid's

treacherous murder, she marries the elderly Fionn mac Cumhaill, whom she had previously rejected and who is responsible for her lover's death. Later interpreters of the story have wrestled with this seemingly contradictory behaviour. Some speculate that Grainne is attracted by the power that marriage to Fionn will accord her (Innes, 1993: 155–6); others depict her as a mother concerned for the welfare of her children after Diarmaid's death.

Lady Gregory once explained her preference for Grainne's story, and her decision to write a play about her rather than another version of the Deirdre story:

> I think I turned to Grania because so many have written about sad, lovely Deirdre, who when overtaken by sorrow made no good battle at the last. Grania had more power of will, and for good or evil twice took the shaping of her life into her own hands. (Quoted in Innes, 1993: 155)

Trevor, whose Irish women are more often cast in the Deirdre role, passive victims of male domination and social circumstance, makes a departure in "August Saturday". His contemporary Grania makes a drastic decision to remedy the childlessness that haunts her otherwise happy marriage. Her circumstances are decidedly not the stuff of myth, however. Grania has lived in the same provincial area all her life, which has become a routine of tennis club, golf course, and social gatherings with lifelong friends. To an outsider, this existence seems both superficial and claustrophobic, but Grania seems content in both her marriage and her friendships. Trevor underlines the contrast between myth and reality, but the story's mood is complex. On one hand, he invests considerable comic irony in the story's setting, for just as the reader begins to connect the Tara Hotel in which Grania and her friends are having dinner to the ancient seat of Irish kings and the mythical Grainne's former home, we are informed that the place is named for the plantation in *Gone With the Wind*, whose characters and the actors who portrayed them on film figure largely in the hotel's decor, a sign of a new encroaching imperialism, American popular culture. Pictures of Vivian Leigh and Clark Gable loom over the dinner conversation, which is comprised mostly of chat about children, jobs and the appearance of an apparent stranger.

Trevor both adopts pieces of the myth and undercuts it. Disparity in age, a key element in the mythical Grainne's distaste for Fionn, is translated into the story of Grania's friend Oliver Duddy, who drinks too much at dinner and makes a nuisance of himself by fussing about his daughter's interest in an older man — of 35! With a delicious touch of irony, Trevor names the independent daughter with a mind of her own Aisling, an ironic reference to the ancient Irish poetic genre which in the eighteenth century often included the political metaphor of a woman awaiting rescue — i.e. Ireland awaiting liberation. Grania herself becomes sexually involved with another man — a one-night stand — because she wants to become pregnant, not because she dislikes her husband, Desmond.

Trevor also invests the story with considerable political irony, for Grania's sexual partner is an Englishman visiting the local Big House. Although he seems to fancy himself a skilled seducer, he does not realise that Grania has chosen *him* — perhaps Trevor's variant on the *geis* (spell) which the mythical Grainne imposed on Diarmaid to compel him to run away with her. The Englishman — and even Grania does not know his name — unwittingly aids this Irish couple, for with the biological predictability one usually associates only with soap operas, Grania becomes pregnant as a result of one sexual encounter, a secret she has concealed for sixteen years, during which she and Desmond have raised a much-beloved daughter. The encounter takes place in the Big House itself, but whatever the Englishman may believe about his easy success with a local married woman, it is Grania who controls the situation. Trevor reverses a familiar pattern here: historically, it was often the colonising English or Big House man who sexualised and often sexually exploited the indigenous Irish.

Given the complex ironies of Trevor's handling of the Grainne story, it is difficult to accept Morrison's contention that the story is an example of "parental failure", noting that "This Englishman may not warrant a name, but he is quite effective as a lover, able to achieve in one night what Grania's husband could not accomplish in 24 years" (1991, 141). Desmond is not a failed father; he is simply not a biological one; the Englishman is not a lover, but rather, convenient for stud purposes.

The tension in the story derives from the fact that the lover has returned to Ireland to attend the funeral of the last Big House survivor, Hetty Prendergast, and plans to settle in the house. Grania conceals her panic at what this return might entail, particularly because her friends are already speculating that the apparently impecunious Englishman might be a good match for one of their financially secure friends who is both widowed and in search of a new home — and the Big House is badly in need of repair. But like her mythical counterpart, Grania does not assume a victim's stance at the end of the story. The discovery of her secret could be potentially catastrophic, ending not in murder but in the emotional wounding of her husband and estrangement from her lifelong friends. In this respect, "August Saturday" is not ironic, for Trevor seems to be suggesting that what unites myth and ordinary life is the passions and affections and betrayals that are endemic to being human. Ultimately, Grania confronts her life without regret, and seems ready to face the consequences of her past.

Not all of the women in *Family Sins* possess Grania's ability to take control of her own life and to face down the consequences. The psychologically self-immolating Ariadne of "In Love with Ariadne" rejects a devoted lover and enters a convent because she is tormented by the memory of her father, an alleged child molester who committed suicide rather than face arrest. In the title story, the gentle Pamela becomes the victim of her self-loathing, sadistic cousin. Maura Brigid Colleary, much as she would like to forgive her unfaithful husband ("A Husband's Return"), lacks the strength to stand up to her hostile family. Kitty of "Honeymoon in Tramore" marries Davy, whom she does not love, because, as she is pregnant by another man in a 1940s rural community, her only other choices are the social stigma of being an unwed mother or getting an illegal abortion, which she is convinced will result in damnation.

Trevor's sympathetic rendering of women's lives is not unique to *Family Sins*. But as well as being a sensitive rendering of constrained lives, this volume reveals the author's growing concern with the issue of Irish identity and Irish self-definition. Trevor challenges the reductive, romanticised images of women that have too long informed Irish literature and visual art at the expense of real Irish women.

Chapter Seven

The Imperial Serial Killer:
Felicia's Journey

Felicia's Journey is the suspense-filled story of a pregnant Irish teenager stalked by a sinister Englishman. When it was published in 1994, it was widely acclaimed both for its linguistic brilliance and its characterisation of a chilling yet pitiable predator. Several of its reviewers described the novel as a "thriller", viewing it as a departure for Trevor, a venture into a previously unplumbed genre. James Bowman described the novel as "this subtlest and most beautifully written of thrillers" (1995, 67); Patricia Craig, though asserting that the novel is not a thriller, still commented that it "teeters on the edge of being [one]" (1994, 37). Viking Penguin, Trevor's publisher, promoted *Felicia's Journey* as a thriller, for not only does the dust jacket of the first American edition cite reviewers who describe the novel as such, it also opines that the novel is "a page-turner that will magnetise fans of Hitchcock and of Ruth Rendell at her most laconically chilling".

The term "thriller" is in itself problematic, for the genre has been variously defined; it has been combined with and separated from the detective story, the mystery, the spy story and other related forms. Julian Symons, finding that "such classifications are more confusing than helpful" (1985, 13), uses the term "sensational literature" (15) to characterise the thriller, the detective story, the suspense novel, et al. And although some practitioners in crime writing have developed distinct classifications for these various genres (Keating, 1982: 30ff), it seems likely that Trevor's reviewers were using the term "thriller" loosely, meaning a novel that produces a state of suspense in its readers, examines extreme psychological states and deals with real or implicit violence.

In fact, *Felicia's Journey* is not a dramatic departure for Trevor: the author has had a lifelong fascination with the thriller: as he noted in an interview for *Paris Review*, his child-hood reading of thrillers was his first inspiration to pursue a career in writing: "I was a great reader of thrillers. When I was ten I wanted to write thrillers" (Stout, 1989–90: 124).

Trevor's early love of what Symons calls "sensational lit-erature" manifests itself in earlier fiction: the revenge-twisted Willie Quinton of *Fools of Fortune*; the self-destructive Rolleston family secret in *The Silence in the Garden*; and the cryptic murders/suicide in "Events at Drimaghleen" are but a few examples. Trevor's works have frequently revealed the violence, the suspense, and the extreme psychological states that one associates with the thriller, the search for meaning and closure that informs detective and mystery stories.

Like numerous other modern and contemporary authors — William Faulkner, Vladimir Nabokov, Jorge Luis Borges, Margaret Atwood, Umberto Eco, John Banville — Trevor blurs the old distinction between "canonical literature" and "popular fiction" by employing the conventions of the thriller/detective story for complex artistic purposes. Yet like the authors mentioned above, Trevor deviates from the tra-ditional detective story, eschewing the triumph of reason and the re-establishment of order that that genre has often en-tailed. Violence effects a permanent disruption of lives, ex-poses the corruption and failure of society, and we are often left knowing only that we know very little. His real literary departure in *Felicia's Journey* is not so much that it employs elements of sensational literature but in *how* they are manipulated into a sustained allegory of Anglo-Irish relations.

Certainly Trevor has linked the thriller and political allegory before — as we have seen, in "Events at Drimaghleen", *The Silence in the Garden*, "Attracta", "Beyond the Pale", and other works. When "Events at Drimaghleen" opens, the three violent deaths have already occurred: the dramatic tension is rooted not in the suspenseful build-up to a shocking climax but rather in the attempts of the McDowd family, the local Garda, and an English journalist to explain the deaths. Similarly, in *The Silence in the Garden*, both murder and attempted murder took place several decades earlier; Trevor directs our attention to the ways in which those crimes continue to blight the lives of the Rollestons and their household. "Attracta" and "Beyond the Pale" connect dreadful acts of violence in time past and time present.

These works also may be read symbolically: the community of Drimaghleen, both living and dead, is victimised by an English journalist's use of reductive stereotypes. *The Silence in the Garden* creates a microcosm of Ireland, intertwining personal tragedy and national history. "Beyond the Pale" and "Attracta" reveal Irish history as a continuum of violence that must be broken.

What sets *Felicia's Journey* apart from Trevor's earlier works is that while he adheres more closely to the sensationalism of the thriller — we follow in the steps of a psychologically disturbed man as he stalks his intended victim and are drawn into the escalating suspense as she attempts to escape him — he does so to construct his subtlest, most deeply ironic reading of Anglo-Irish relations.

Using crime as a frame for exploring issues of identity, both personal and cultural, is a frequent strategy employed by such diverse post-colonial writers as Ngugi wa Thiong'o,

Nadine Gordimer, Margaret Atwood, and Bharati Mukherjee. The personal and social disruptions occasioned by violent crime challenge the characters' sense of self and often expose long-buried faultlines within the society. In *Felicia's Journey*, Trevor challenges the cultural myths that have shaped both Felicia and her stalker, Hilditch. Her life has been grounded in an Irish nationalist mythology that exalts imaginary women and oppresses real ones; his sense of self is rooted in a British imperial ideal that Trevor soundly debunks by novel's end.

Pregnant Felicia journeys to England to find the father of her child, a young man from her hometown who is now, unbeknownst to her, a soldier in the British Army. Profoundly naïve and stolidly trusting that Johnny Lysaght loves her, she leaves Ireland armed only with a stolen portion of her great-grandmother's savings and the vague information that Johnny works in a lawnmower factory north of Birmingham — he has never divulged his address. But England for this Irish girl becomes a place of Dantean ferocity, her circular wanderings leading her deeper into terrifying evil.

The evils Trevor depicts are all too grounded in contemporary reality, from the trash and graffiti-soured streets to the ugly industrial estate where "Business is in all directions, buying and selling, disposal and acquisition, discount for cash" (*FJ*, 14), to the denizens of the town by night: the homeless, the addicted, the rejected. Trevor exposes the legacy of the Industrial Revolution and the failure of capitalist "progress" to produce the ameliorist society that some eminent Victorians once envisioned. His description of the town in which the novel is set echoes Dickens, who so eloquently castigated the effects of both industry and capitalism and for whose works Trevor has expressed admiration.

> There are no hills. Against a grey sky, tall bleak chimneys belch out their own hot clouds. Factories seem like fortresses, their towers protecting ancient

> realms of iron and wealth. Terracotta everywhere
> has blackened to the insistent local sheen. The lie of
> the land is lost beneath a weight of purpose, its natu-
> ral idiosyncrasy stifled, contours pressed away. (34)

At the centre of Trevor's contemporary Inferno is Joseph
Ambrose Hilditch, a superficially genial, enormously obese
catering manager whose secret life is the befriending and
probably murder of lonely and desperate young women. As in
"Events at Drimaghleen", Trevor withholds information. We
never know for sure what happens to the young women
Hilditch befriends, though we are led to believe that the man's
imagined collection of photographs of young women, which
he calls "Memory Lane", is in fact a gallery of murder victims.

A brilliantly conceived character, at once monstrous and
pathetic, Hilditch is also linked to England's imperial past. His
vast home is located at No. 3, Duke of Wellington Road —
named for the Irish-born yet Irish-scorning military defender
of British colonial interest. The house itself contains vestiges
of colonialism — it once belonged to a tea merchant, and its
furnishings include "ivory trinkets", "secondhand Indian car-
pets", and "Twenty mezzotints of South African military
scenes" (7). Hilditch himself suffers the lifelong disappointment of being thwarted in his desire for a career in the British
Army, a vocation instilled in him by one of his mother's lovers, Uncle Wilf, a former soldier who once informed him that
"'The Black and Tans should have sorted that island out . . .
only unfortunately they held back for humane reasons'" (149).

Hilditch calculatingly renders the hapless Felicia dependent upon him, and as Patrick McGrath has observed, "Never
did spider more hungrily anticipate fly" (1995, 22). Having
secretly stolen her money, he renders her destitute, and
after nights spent in an eccentric religious community, a Sal-
vation Army shelter, and finally in a derelict building inhabited by transients, she returns to Hilditch's untender

mercies. He persuades her that having an abortion is the best solution to her predicament, assuring her that her pregnancy will evoke disgust in her lover and bring humiliation to her family. But after acceding to Hilditch's wishes, Felicia, a Catholic, is tormented by guilt.

The Ireland that Felicia leaves behind bears vestiges of a colonial past — an economy so depressed that when the meat-processing factory in which she works shuts down, there is little other prospect for employment. Her lover, Johnny Lysaght, has long since abandoned Ireland because he has no future there. Felicia, motherless since childhood, lives in a working-class family, her father the tender caretaker of her great-grandmother, widow of a patriot killed in the Irish struggle for independence.

Elsewhere in his fiction, Trevor has exploded the Irish nationalists' reductive mythologising of women: this old woman, whom Felicia's father venerates as a widow in the cause of Irish freedom, is senile, incontinent and querulous. So caught up is he in his own mythologising that Felicia's father fails to see his real daughter, who was named for a woman killed on the barricades in 1916. He encourages her to settle for a part-time job as a cleaner so that she may help to tend the old lady; when he suspects Felicia is pregnant, he calls her "hooer"; when he hears rumours that Johnny Lysaght is a British soldier he threatens to disown her. Particularly pointed is Trevor's description of the scrapbooks Felicia's father so painstakingly maintains for her uncomprehending great-grandmother, books filled with mementoes of Ireland's struggle for independence. In one of his characteristic ironic juxtapositions, Trevor quotes de Valera's famous words:

> "The Ireland which we have dreamed of would be the home of a people who valued material wealth only as the basis of right living, of a people who were satisfied with frugal comfort and devoted their

> leisure to the things of the spirit; a land whose coun-
> tryside would be bright with cosy homesteads,
> whose fields would be joyous with the sounds of in-
> dustry, with the romping of sturdy children, the con-
> tests of athletic youths, the laughter of comely
> maidens; whose firesides would be forums for the
> wisdom of old age. It would, in a word, be the home
> of a people living the life that God desires men
> should live." (26–7)

Immediately after this passage is cited, Felicia responds nega-
tively to her father's inquiry about her job prospects. Felicia
is no "comely maiden"; her financial and personal worries
leave little room for the "things of the spirit"; senility, not the
"wisdom of old age", inhabits her house. Ireland's partial independence has not brought Felicia's family the ideal life that
de Valera envisioned: their legacy is poverty, unemployment,
and a dreary quotidian reality. Further, just as in the early
years of independence Irish women were stunned to discover that they had been betrayed by their male compatriots,
denied a place at the political table in the new nation, Felicia's
nationalist father assumes that a life of family caretaking and
part-time menial work is adequate for his daughter.

Further, Felicia has been denied knowledge about her
own body and sexuality. When she encounters Johnny
Lysaght, she has never even kissed a boy before; her Catholic upbringing has left her so unschooled in reproductive
matters that she cannot tell that, despite his reassurances,
Johnny has taken no precautions against pregnancy. Her
sexuality has been kept in check, and when she deviates
from the code she has been taught, she is guilt-ridden, fearful of the shame her pregnancy will bring on the family and
imagining the jeers of her more worldly-wise friends.

When Felicia abandons her unpropitious setting for England, she is in effect colonised by Hilditch. As Liam Harte
and Lance Pettitt have noted,

> Felicia suffers a double oppression on account of her
> gender and nationality. In Ireland she is a victim of
> patriarchal nationalism; in England she is oppressed
> by the embodiment of a malign residual colonialism.
> (2000, 73)

Protesting that he has only her welfare at heart, Hilditch
renders her increasingly powerless. Her reluctance to become dependent upon him elicits anger and sorrow at her
ingratitude, reminiscent of Victorian England's reaction to
Irish bids for independence, which often entailed similar
emotional responses: the Irish were accused of disloyalty,
treachery, and thanklessness in the face of England's alleg-
edly benevolent despotism. Hilditch's seemingly unquench-
able appetite for food — he cannot see a comestible
without sating the desire to make it his — is likewise a
darkly humorous link with England's colonial rapacity. As
Gail Caldwell observed in her review of the novel:

> "*Felicia's Journey* may be about the battle on the high
> plains between light and darkness, but it also hints at
> a more earth-bound sovereignty: The silent images
> of the Black and Tans hang in the shadows, and as
> Hilditch tries to impose upon his quarry the same
> well-intentioned tyranny Ireland has known from
> Britain, one can't help feeling a kind of psychic impe-
> rialism at play. (1995, 49)

Likewise evocative of Anglo-Irish history are Hilditch's attempts to "colonise" Felicia's Catholicism. He exerts psychological pressure to persuade her to violate her religious
principles by having an abortion. Having already rendered
her financially desperate by stealing her money, he now assures her that Johnny will feel "trapped" by the pregnancy,
that it will bring shame upon her family. Asserting that his
wider experience of the world renders him a knowledgeable

advisor, he tempts her with the promise of financial assistance, entices her with the assurance that the abortion will end her troubles, render her a "free spirit". Just as in Ireland Felicia was kept ignorant of her sexuality, her body in effect controlled by her family's religious codes, Hilditch, like her father, attempts to impose his own will upon her body.

When Felicia does indeed have the abortion, the effects are devastating. Her normally quiet, even stolid façade shatters, and she alarms Hilditch with her sobbing and shouting. Guilt-ridden, she dreams of her dead mother's sorrowful reproaches, of her own attempts to beg forgiveness from a blind-eyed statue of the Virgin Mary. Her trauma prefigures her ultimate mental disintegration.

The abortion is for Hilditch an assertion of his power and a bolstering of his shaky self-esteem. He enjoys taking Felicia to the clinic because it allows him, an unattractive, middle-aged man, to pose as the father of a teenager's child, to pretend that he is desirable. Deliberately drawing attention to himself in the waiting room, he makes frequent reference to his "girlfriend" and is gratified by the speculative glances he receives. In fact, being seen with young women is the heart of Hilditch's sexual fantasy. Squeamish about sex itself, his recurring desire is to be believed lovable.

Trevor finally turns the tables on this latter-day coloniser, however. Felicia escapes the fate of the other young women ensconced in Hilditch's "Memory Lane", who have presumably become his murder victims, and the escape hastens Hilditch's destruction. He becomes obsessed with finding her, and unlike his previous "friends", consistently referred to by their names, Felicia becomes the "Irish girl", and Hilditch describes his feelings in decidedly colonial terms: ". . . he awakes with the eccentric notion that the Irish girl has invaded him, as territory is invaded" (179). He is a haunted man: having lost his ravenous appetite and his pleasure in a once-loved job, he ultimately hangs himself in his kitchen.

Before Hilditch's death, he is assailed by other reminders of a collapsed Empire: haunted by the memory of Felicia, he changes places with her: just as Felicia wearily trudged the streets of an English town searching for her lover, Hilditch roams those same streets, the scenes of his childhood, in search of Felicia; he also tracks down Johnny Lysaght, an object of envy not only because he has been Felicia's lover but also because the same British Army that rejected Hilditch for medical reasons has willingly accepted the young Irishman. But the streets of Hilditch's childhood have changed, changed utterly:

> He goes to places he hasn't visited in years, to the neighbourhoods the Indians or Pakistanis have taken over. The Boroda Express offers the variety stars of India. . . . The Wool Shop he remembers, stockers of Sirdar Wools and Bairnswear, is the Rupali Boutique. (179–80)

These same streets echo with reminders that the formerly colonised are now asserting their own brand of economic imperialism — Hilditch notes establishments selling Kentucky Fried Chicken and Coca Cola; storefronts blast out the music of Michael Jackson and Sheena Easton.

Finally, the catalyst for Hilditch's self-destruction is herself a colonial — the eccentric Miss Calligary, a West Indian woman who proselytises for the Gathering, the religious community where Felicia once sought refuge. Relentless in her determination to gather Hilditch in to her community's promises of paradise, Calligary unwittingly stirs up Hilditch's own unbearable past as a sexually abused child whose profound sense of shame has filled him with self-loathing and a conviction of his own unlovableness.

Under Trevor's ironic scrutiny, the oft-idealised image of the British Empire collapses. Hilditch, devoted to that ideal, is a man both bedevilled by and utterly committed to the past. Resisting what he sees as the vulgarity of contemporary life, he owns neither telephone nor television, preferring the company of his old gramophone records.

As in previous fiction, Trevor uses popular songs to reflect his characters' self-delusions. Not only does the reactionary Hilditch prefer music from the 1930s, '40s and '50s, his favourites underline the difference between his genial façade and his ghastly psyche. He delights in the breeziness of "Chattanooga Choo Choo" and "Five Foot Two, Eyes of Blue"; favours the sentimentality of "Charmaine", "Stella by Starlight", and "Besame Mucho". Punctuating his slow campaign to conquer Felicia are "I Got It Bad and That Ain't Good", "I Can't Help Falling in Love with You", and "You Belong to Me", but the surrender to passion expressed in those torch songs is here used ironically to evoke Hilditch's obsession and his detachment from reality.

And Hilditch is indeed a man who cannot bear too much reality. Noting the apparently frustrated and unhappy people on the streets of his town, he reflects:

> There is so much of that, Mr Hilditch considers as he makes his way back to his car, so much violence in the world, so much prickliness. *Keep your Distance!* a sticker rudely orders on the back window of a car. *Surfers Do it Standing Up!* another informs. *I Want Madonna!* a T-shirt message asserts. Mr Hilditch finds it all unattractive. (41)

He is dismayed by the violence and cruelty of contemporary life, and reflects on the sensational news stories he has read about child abuse, the rape of elderly women, teenage girls "set alight on city wastelands" (98). Yet Hilditch never connects his own stalking and probably murder of the vulnerable with such horrors. With a streak of decidedly black humour, Trevor notes that this predator goes to see the film *Basic Instinct* but "finds it unpleasant" (171), staying for the end only because he wants his money's worth.

Hilditch at times embodies the qualities of the idealised Victorian gentleman credited with building the Empire: he is courteous, values hard work, venerates ancestors, and adopts a protective attitude toward women, including his deceased mother. Yet these very qualities are deceptive: Hilditch's courtesy and gallantry are employed to lure vulnerable young women into danger; the ancestors who grace Hilditch's walls and the colonial artefacts that fill his rooms are not family heirlooms but rather Hilditch's own purchases. His adored mother becomes his seducer, turning to her son for sexual gratification when other lovers have abandoned her, among them Uncle Wilf, Hilditch's childhood hero, whose grandiose image collapses. For Hilditch bitterly realises Uncle Wilf's treachery in filling him with impossible dreams of military glory, presenting himself as the boy's "guide" and "friend" when in fact what he was really after was "Bit on the side, until he didn't fancy it any more and never came back again" (200). After Uncle Wilf's abandonment, Mrs Hilditch begins her sexual abuse of her son, left unprotected by his "guide" and "friend".

Hilditch, the superficially genial catering manager, is a tormented soul and a dangerous sexual predator. By associating him symbolically with the Empire, Trevor reminds us of the greed, violence and abuse of power that were the dark side of Britain's glory days as an imperial power. By examining the poisonous effects that imperial myths have had upon Hilditch's psyche, Trevor explores, as he did in "The News from Ireland", the deleterious effects of colonisation upon the coloniser, commented upon by such post-colonial critics as Ashis Nandy and Albert Memmi. Finally, by exposing Hilditch's carefully constructed world as bogus — Uncle

Wilf is a fraud, the colonial artefacts in Hilditch's house are in effect a stage setting gleaned from jumble sales and junk shops — Trevor snaps a warp thread in the tattered fabric of Victorian jingoism.

Felicia eludes Hilditch and is transformed into one of Trevor's familiar figures: a mentally unbalanced woman of surpassing goodness and forgiveness. She comes to pity not only Hilditch's victims but Hilditch himself; she does not return to Ireland, where, unbeknownst to her, her great-grandmother has died and her father is tormented by grief and remorse at his daughter's absence. Her entire life has become a journey, as she wanders homelessly from city to city, touched occasionally by the kindness of strangers.

By novel's end, both Felicia and Hilditch have been freed of the myths that controlled them, but the cost is dear. Hilditch despairingly kills himself; Felicia joins the legions of England's homeless, albeit having gained "a degree of spiritual enlightenment" (Harte and Pettitt, 2000: 76). Ultimately Trevor extends compassion to all — Hilditch, his victims, Felicia herself — demonstrating in this novel his lifelong concern with the ways in which human beings damage themselves and others. But in his Irish fiction, that exploration of damage has taken an increasingly post-colonial turn: colonialism and its attendant oppressions, political and economic, blunt human sensibilities, poison human relationships. And though Trevor has often resisted a political interpretation of his fiction, when *Felicia's Journey* was published, he conceded in an interview:

> I'm more interested in people as people than as people with nationalities tacked on to them. . . . But anyone who reads something like that into the work is not necessarily wrong. If he sees it that way, it's another kind of truth. (Graeber, 1995: 22)

Ironically, when Atom Egoyan decided to make a film of Trevor's novel, he removed much of its commentary on Anglo-Irish relations. Egoyan has noted that he met with Trevor and shared drafts of the screenplay with him (Porton, 1999: 41). The cultural tensions of the novel intrigued him, but he differed from Trevor in interpreting them. Asserting that the Ireland of Trevor's novel is no longer in evidence — "Ireland is very prosperous and a lot of the towns are all tarted up for the tourist industry" (39) — and disagreeing with what he sees as the author's "reductive" psychology, Egoyan imposed his own vision on *Felicia's Journey*, producing a brilliant film, but one that diverges considerably from Trevor's text.

Egoyan's perception that Felicia must re-invent herself, not be enslaved by the myths of the past, is certainly aligned with the intellectual preoccupations of many contemporary Irish intellectuals, concerned as they are with the thorny question of Irish identity. But Trevor's novel, evolving as it does from a lifelong preoccupation with the cultural collisions between England and Ireland, explodes the myths that have hobbled both nations.

Chapter Eight

Roads Not Taken:
The Hill Bachelors

Half of the stories in Trevor's latest collection, *The Hill Bachelors*, are not only set in Ireland but also explore the author's favourite Irish themes — the legacy of the Troubles, the confinement of provincial Ireland, the confronting of unsettling truths. Sombre and elegiac, these stories both revisit familiar themes and subtly shift the ground. Out of melancholy, even bleak circumstances, many of the characters in these recent Irish stories unearth the fragile hope that change is indeed possible. Gone is the historical determinism of Trevor's early Troubles stories; lingering is the possibility that the Irish can re-imagine their lives, extricate themselves from the disabling past.

"Of the Cloth", discussed in a previous chapter, reveals how a young priest and an elderly Church of Ireland minister are able to move beyond sectarian divides, suggesting that an easing of the religious tensions that have divided the communities is possible.

"The Mourning" and the as-yet-uncollected "Big Bucks" revisit a traditional Irish theme — emigration — by adding a less familiar twist: staying home. Trevor's own reluctant emigration in the face of economic exigency has attuned him to the pain of many generations of Irish people forced by circumstances to leave home, sometimes with little hope of return. The heartbreak of departure is a familiar Irish theme; less commonly do writers examine the return to Ireland. One thinks of Gar O'Donnell's well-meaning but silly Aunt Lizzie in *Philadelphia, Here I Come!* or the title character of its companion piece, *The Loves of Cass McGuire*. Both returned emigrants have become alien in their own homeland, their newfound outspokenness and effusiveness a family embarrassment.

In "The Mourning", Liam Pat Brogan, a good-hearted, rather unintelligent young man, decides that England can offer him better opportunities than his current job as a manual labourer. Like many emigrants, though, Liam Pat finds England lonely and unfriendly, himself the victim of his boss's anti-Irish prejudice. Befriended by the seemingly sympathetic Feeny, Liam Pat reluctantly agrees to aid Feeny's Republican cause by planting a bomb. Feeny begins by easing Liam Pat's loneliness, ends by persuading him that he will be a hero in the mould of Michael Collins. Liam Pat, assured that no one will be injured, carries the bomb on board a bus. But in a moment of revelation, he recalls another young man on a similar mission, an untimely explosion. Realising that he has been chosen to complete the dead man's aborted mission, Liam Pat decides to throw the bomb in a river and return home to Ireland. Although his initial motivation is fear for his personal safety, he ultimately identifies with and mourns the dead boy, knowing that he himself might have come to a similar end, that he himself was similarly manipulated by Feeny and his cohorts. Naïve and a bit slow-witted, Liam Pat nevertheless acquires dignity in his final decision to keep that mourning alive. Knowing that he must keep silent, aware that returning to Ireland will mean a lifetime of low-level construction jobs with no real hope of advancement, Liam Pat chooses peace, chooses home.

Without denying the injustices of Anglo-Irish relations and anti-Irish bigotry, Trevor nevertheless suggests that violence is no answer. Liam Pat, as Feeny well knows, is a perfect candidate for his plan: simple, lacking in self-confidence, homesick, and warm-hearted, the younger man is vulnerable to sympathy, attracted by the notion of joining the ranks of Ireland's national heroes. Trevor suggests that this predictable situation can have an alternative ending: Liam Pat does not have to join the cycle of violence, just as he does not have to join the faceless ranks of Irish emigrants in England.

Not surprisingly, melancholy images of emigration abound in Irish literature. Liam O'Flaherty in "Going into Exile" summons the poignant image of Michael Feeney breaking a piece of whitewash as a memento of the home he is leaving for America; in *Philadelphia, Here I Come!*, Gar O'Donnell's ambivalence about emigrating is emphasised by Friel's dividing the character into two separate roles.

In both these works, and in the historical reality that they reflect, emigration is both driven by economic imperatives and fraught with emotional upheaval: the uncertain promise of prosperity in America is purchased at the high price of losing one's cultural and familiar identity.

In the nearly 40 years since the premiere of *Philadelphia, Here I Come!*, emigration has continued to preoccupy Irish life and Irish literature. The 1990s economic surge nicknamed the "Celtic Tiger" enabled many young Irish people to escape the inevitable emigration for economic survival; nevertheless, for many years, there was growing concern on both sides of the Atlantic about the exodus of the young from Ireland. Naturally, Irish and Irish-American writers have continued to voice the ambivalence that attends emigration and resettlement, the opportunities lost, found and revealed to be chimerical.

In the 1997 short story "Big Bucks", published in *The New Yorker* but as yet uncollected, William Trevor explores the complexities of contemporary emigration. Fina and John Michael, an engaged couple contemplating leaving Ireland in hopes of a more prosperous future in America, are not *compelled* to emigrate. Remaining in Ireland is not impossible; emigration to America is not inevitable. Fina's awareness of that fact and John Michael's refusal to accept it provokes their estrangement.

Like much of Trevor's recent writing about Ireland, "Big Bucks" is not only marked by verisimilitude but is also a work that lends itself to an allegorical reading. The couple's story is both a particularised account of their individual dilemma and a symbolic reading of a larger problem.

Fina and John Michael live on the seacoast, where he has been working as a fisherman. The perils of that way of life have hit home, as John Michael's father was drowned when his son was only an infant. Fina works in her parents' half-and-half, both grocery and pub, in a village where she and her fiancé are the only remaining young people. Both possess modest prospects for the future if they remain in Ireland. Fina will inherit her parents' shop because neither of her brothers wants it; John Michael will inherit his uncle's derelict farm, whose rehabilitation, though daunting, is not impossible.

As is sometimes true of aspiring emigrants, real and fictional, Fina and John Michael have patched together a picture of America based on unreliable sources. American television casts its allure even over their tiny fishing village:

> They watched America, they heard its voices. Its ballgame heroes battled, rigid in their padding and their helmets. Steam swirled above the nighttime gratings of its city streets. Legs wide, eyes dead, gangsters splayed their fingers on precinct walls. ("Big Bucks", 70)

Fina is attracted not by the hope of easy money, but by the exotic television images that contrast to her all-too-familiar community. Only later does she come to realise that she agreed to emigrate only because she didn't believe that such an eventuality would actually present itself.

John Michael, who has delayed his departure until after his ailing mother's death, has been much more susceptible to the promise of "big bucks", a phrase frequently on the lips of Bat Quinn, a regular at the family pub. Quinn's conversation is peppered with tales of success, all his acquaintances who struck it rich in America.

But Bat Quinn has no firsthand knowledge of America, and after John Michael's departure, he, too, is subjected to Quinn's mythmaking. The couple's original plan — that John Michael get himself settled in America, return for their wedding and take Fina to their new home — unravels. After several months, John Michael has a low-paying job, a one-room apartment, and a new awareness of the Byzantine complexities of immigration law. Yet when Fina informs Quinn that John Michael is working in a laundry, the older man asserts to her, "'There were big bucks in the laundry business, no doubt about it'", but announces to the pub customers that "'John Michael Gallagher was in charge of the shirts of the President of the United States'" (70).

When John Michael's lack of a green card makes it impossible for him to return to Ireland to marry Fina, she comes to the painful realisation that she will never accede to his wishes and join him in America. She recognises that she and John Michael are part of a long historical continuum:

> It had never been easy. Not since the Famine years, the first great exodus from the land, the ships called coffin ships. Chance had always played a part: in the journey, in what was there after it. There was always uncertainty, always misfortune and desperation and

failure. You knew where you were if you stayed, you
know the worst. (72)

Fina believes she lacks the courage to start a new life with
John Michael and recognises in the bombastic Bat Quinn,
whom she had previously disliked, a kindred spirit: he, too,
had been afraid to leave Ireland.

But Fina undergoes a deeper epiphany: the realisation
that familiarity and long acquaintance had created the illusion
of intimacy between herself and John Michael. They were
the sole children waiting for the school bus, close companions all their lives; both are modest and gentle. They even
resemble each other physically. Though she has wanted to
marry John Michael all her life, she now realises that "Close
to one another, she and John Michael had sometimes hardly
seemed two different people. Apart, they were aware of the
insistence that they were" (73).

"Big Bucks" is an understated, touching story with one
of Trevor's characteristically sympathetic female protagonists. But, like much of Trevor's recent fiction about Ireland,
the story also operates on an allegorical level, revealing
Trevor's increasingly post-colonial slant. Yet whereas
Trevor's previous postcolonial fiction has treated Ireland's
colonial relationship with England, "Big Bucks" criticises Ireland's economic and cultural colonisation at the hands of the
United States.

As young adults, Fina and John Michael are seduced by
the slick images on American television, but America's intrusion into their lives began much earlier. Fina recalls her
boredom as a schoolgirl when she was required to learn
seemingly endless facts about the US — geography, history,
and natural resources.

This Irish schoolgirl possesses a knowledge of America
that few Americans could boast of; further, American
schoolchildren have never had to be so well-versed in Irish

history and geography. Fina's recollections of her schoolmaster's cramming her with facts, like an Irish version of Dickens's Mr Gradgrind, have had one benefit, for her grounding in facts has made her more resistant than is John Michael to Bat Quinn's grandiose stories.

America's economic and cultural inroads into Ireland have indirectly caused John Michael to reject his own homeland, symbolised by the young man's refusal of the land his uncle offers to him. When Fina visits the farm, she calmly takes in every inch of mouldy wallpaper, bad wiring and collapsing ceiling. Without romanticising the place, she longs to reclaim it, and her reflection that a backhoe could remove the rocks that prevent the land from being ploughed is Trevor's signal that Fina is rooted in reality and the present, not engaging in romantic illusions. She realises sadly that when the uncle dies the farm will become completely derelict, as John Michael is emotionally detached from it.

When "Big Bucks" appeared in *The New Yorker*, the table of contents described it as being about "the romance of not going to America". Though the word "romance" is misleading, it is certainly true that Trevor raises the possibility that remaining in Ireland can be a viable option. By the end of the story, John Michael seems in fact worse off than when he started. He has moved from a close-knit community to the anonymity of an American city; coming from a culture that for pressing historical reasons has long valued a plot of one's own, he has rejected the opportunity of owning land. His expectations of "big bucks" have been reduced to the overtime he makes at the laundry; he fills his hours with work because he is poorly paid and his life in America has seemingly little else to offer him.

Fina, though the more realistic of the two, does in fact retain a fragment of romance at the end. Though she has no illusions that her life in Ireland will change, she believes that her decision to remain is the right one:

> The long companionship, their future planned, their passion and their embraces were marked in memory with a poignancy from which the sting was drawn: fear was not always bad. He would come back and they would walk again on the strand, neither of them mentioning the fragility of love, or that destruction had been averted when they were young. (73)

William Trevor is not prone to nostalgia in his fiction, and is well aware that the Ireland he knew in the 1940s is not contemporary Ireland. Yet it is possible that, at age 75, and in light of more promising economic news from Ireland, he has asked himself "What if?" and granted his characters an option he did not have: remaining at home.

In the title story of *The Hill Bachelors*, Trevor gives a new texture to familiar Irish terrain: the visceral link between people and land. In Irish history's long chronicle of dispossession, of precarious tenantry and subdivided fields, the desire for ownership coupled with the cruel loss of home has been a fact of life and a recurring motif in Irish literature. It is at the heart of the Big House tradition; it receives one of its most chilling treatments in John B. Keane's *The Field*.

In "The Hill Bachelors", as in the earlier "The Ballroom of Romance", the land has become more of a burden than a blessing. Returned home for his father's funeral, Paulie realises that as the only unmarried sibling, he is expected to return to the remote family farm to help his widowed mother, to become one of the many "hill bachelors", unable to attract any woman to such a lonely place.

Trevor carefully avoids the predictable or the stereotypical. Paulie's mother is neither possessive nor guilt-inducing; as is true throughout his fiction, Trevor resists Irish female stereotypes. She offers to leave the farm or to get by with the assistance of neighbours; she does not wish to compel her son to give up his own life for hers.

Paulie's siblings, having long left the land behind them, assume, with the sometime arrogance of the married-with-children toward the single, that he doesn't have much of a life anyway. In fact, despite the story's modern setting, the family has scattered as surely as they might have in the nineteenth century. Though one brother lives in Boston, other siblings remain in Ireland — yet Paulie has never met his siblings' children. Paulie's decision to come home is a weighty one, entailing the loss of the woman he loves, who has no intention of living in such an isolated place. As the months go on, it is apparent that Paulie's search for a wife will be fruitless.

Trevor invests the story with subtle psychology. Paulie literally steps into his father's shoes (or wellington boots, that is) — a father who viewed him as inconsequential. His mother's terse recollection bespeaks the father's quiet cruelty: "Frances had been the favourite, then Mena; Kevin was approved of because he was reliable; Aidan was the first-born. Paulie hadn't been often mentioned" (*HB*, 228). Yet it is clear that Paulie is a skilled and hardworking farmer who will make more of the land than his father had. His newfound pride of place compels him to reject a neighbour's offer to buy the land and thus free him from his family obligations: Paulie envisions the farm's becoming derelict in the neighbour's hands.

Trevor takes pains not to sugar-coat Paulie's decision to remain, even in the event of his mother's death. His will be a lonely life, but it is the life he chooses:

> Guilt was misplaced, goodness hardly came into it. Her widowing and the mood of a capricious time were not of consequence, no more than a flicker in the scheme of things that had always been there. Enduring, unchanging, the hills had waited for him, claiming one of their own. (245)

The Hill Bachelors also provides a new perspective on Trevor's examination of Ireland's ongoing political strife. "Low Sunday", set in 1950s Ireland, depicts a family frozen in time by a ghastly act of violence; "Against the Odds", set in contemporary Northern Ireland, renders the encounter between an ageing con woman and a lonely farmer into a symbolic reading of the struggle for peace.

Philippa and Tom have personally witnessed Ireland's civil war and the founding of the Republic of Ireland, but the pride and pleasure this sister and brother take in that experience is coupled with an accompanying personal tragedy: the accidental killing of their parents by a shell-shocked soldier. Now adults approaching middle age, they live together quietly, bolstered by their familiar communal rituals. Gentle and affectionate toward each other, they are nevertheless paralysed by the family tragedy, evidenced in their private fantasies. Despite their historical distance, Tom feels personally connected to Robert Emmet, leader of the abortive rebellion in 1803 and long revered as an Irish national hero, and his fiancée, Sarah Curran. "In loving because she could not help herself, Sarah too had been a casualty of chance, beyond the battlefield yet left to bear the agony of scars you could not see. They hanged defiant Robert Emmet" (113). In contrast, Philippa fantasises about the future, about a time when she will liberate Tom from his feelings of responsibility toward her by moving out on her own. In her dream, Tom will marry; she will become a cherished aunt. Yet it is quite clear that nothing will change; the trauma of the past, however distant, is still palpable.

The title of the story is the name accorded in the liturgical calendar to the first Sunday after Easter, doubly significant here. In liturgical terms, Low Sunday is somewhat anticlimactic, following as it does the most joyous of Christian holy days. Easter of course also lent its name to the 1916 rebellion which, although its organisers were defeated and compelled to surrender, resulting in the execution of the majority of them, was a catalyst for Ireland's later achievement of independence. Similarly, Tom and Philippa take pride in the independence of their country, but acknowledge that 1950s Ireland is a tame place in contrast to the revolutionary past.

> They rejoiced in all that had come about and even took pride in their accidental closeness to the revolution as it had happened. They had been in at a nation's birth, had later experienced its childhood years, unprosperous and ordinary and undramatic. That a terrible beauty had transformed the land they had not noticed. (108)

Trevor's echoing of Yeats's "terrible beauty" from "Easter 1916" is significant here, for the siblings live in a time warp, their own solitary, sequestered world, oblivious to the dramatic changes around them. More like a married couple than brother and sister, they are symbolically, and very likely literally, incestuous, so tied to their shared past that they are incapable of a psychologically healthier future. On Low Sunday, apparently the anniversary of their parents' killing, Philippa flashes back to a time when her older brother shielded her from the horror that had taken place in their own home.

> Only Low Sunday held them in its thrall, her head pressed into the wool of his jersey, his voice not letting her look. Pity for his romantic ghosts still kept the moment at bay; she had her fantasy of the future. Fragments of intuition were their conversation, real beneath the unreal words. No one else would understand: tomorrow, she would once more know that. (120)

Once Low Sunday has passed, so too has all hope that Philippa will make the necessary move to help them get on with their lives. Like the Middletons in "The Distant Past", the two will be trapped in a past that continues to define them. And like the Rollestons in *The Silence in the Garden*, the siblings' sterile, paralysed lives are ultimately pointless, a terrible waste.

In contrast, in "Against the Odds", Trevor holds out the possibility that people can extricate themselves from their personal and public pasts. Paralleling the story of two emotionally wounded people with the signing of the Belfast Agreement, the story is a poignant account of two people's fragile attempts to transcend the past and a guardedly optimistic parable about the prospect of lasting peace in Northern Ireland.

As "Against the Odds" opens, and we are informed that the protagonist is from Belfast, has a criminal record, and is using an assumed name, it is easy to conclude that she may be involved in political, even terrorist activity. However, Trevor quickly dispels those assumptions, and his story is anything but predictable.

In fact, the woman who uses the name "Mrs Kincaid" has a purely personal agenda for her con games. However, as the story takes place just after the signing of the Belfast Agreement, she and all the other characters are drawn into the fragile hope that their society may indeed see peace:

> Mrs Kincaid had not herself suffered more than inconvenience during the years of conflict; the trouble in her life had been a personal one. Yet the havoc that occurred with such weary repetition and for so long had naturally impinged; she would be glad to see its end. (181)

Though much of Mrs Kincaid's story is withheld by Trevor, we do know that she is 60 but attempts to pass for younger;

that she knows the territory of all Six Counties intimately yet retains a lasting affection for her hometown, Belfast; and that she has never recovered from being duped out of her inheritance by a con man who professed to love her. The £84,000 she had acquired from the sale of inherited property vanished with her fiancé, and though Trevor is reticent about many details of her life, we learn that Mrs Kincaid acquires money by playing on people's trust. Telling herself that she must be philosophical about her loss, she nevertheless cannot escape the damage this betrayal has done her:

> In her business activities, she did not seek vengeance but instead sought to accumulate what was rightfully hers, keeping her accounts in a small red notebook, always with the hope that one day she would not have to do so, that her misfortune in the past would at last free her from its thrall. (188)

Her choices have condemned her to a life of living in furnished rented rooms, of assuming an inoffensive, nondescript appearance so as not to draw suspicion — and, one suspects, of many lonely days and nights. Though she does not at first intend to do so, she cultivates the interest of Mr Blakely, a turkey farmer whose own security has been cruelly shattered: his wife and daughter were killed in a car bombing, a case of mistaken identity. Trevor carefully omits details: we do not know who is responsible for the murders, only that Blakely received a prompt call of apology and that wreaths were sent to the funeral. Like Mrs Kincaid, he evinces no bitterness, no anger, yet the life he leads is surely a lonely one.

Mrs Kincaid slowly wins Blakely's trust. Yet when Blakely, by nature a shy, self-effacing man, suggests a more permanent arrangement, he is stunned by her refusal. Arguing that she has nothing to call her own, that Blakely knows nothing about her, Mrs Kincaid subtly convinces him to write her a cheque for £2,000. Asserting that she will never cash the cheque, that it will be proof of their mutual trust, she persuades him that they must separate for two months, and sets up a time and date when they will meet. She promptly returns to Belfast and cashes the cheque.

Though it is clear that Mrs Kincaid has engaged in this particular con before, she cannot put Blakely out of her mind, thinking that she might have married him, thinking that she could write and apologise, feeling confident that she will be able to find the appropriate words. For his part, Blakely is disappointed and saddened, but neither angry nor despairing.

And in fact, Trevor lets us know that there *is* cause for optimism, for as the story ends, Mrs Kincaid has written her letter, and there is hope that these two wounded, lonely people will arrive at their own truce.

"Against the Odds" is a touching story about the complexities of forgiveness and of making new beginnings. Yet Trevor's story is not only a sympathetic tale of two bruised souls but also a parable for the Belfast Agreement.

The signing of the Agreement touches the lives of all of the characters in the story, and Trevor captures the mixed feelings that greeted it in Northern Ireland. Mrs Kincaid is delighted, and expresses her joy to a busdriver, who responds, "'There's maybe something in their bits of paper . . . We'll see'" (181–2), for "whatever agreements had been reached, whatever pledges given, there were gunmen who had not gone away, who still possessed their armoury and were used to calling the tune" (182). Blakely's own tragedy has rendered him more pessimistic than Mrs Kincaid: he believes "The men of violence were still in charge, no doubt about it" (184). When he first meets Mrs Kincaid, he responds cautiously to her questions, and she perceives the inherent reticence of a Northern Irish man: "not knowing about her, not knowing which foot she dug with, as her father used to say, he held back" (186).

Suggestions of the fragility of peace linger in Mrs Kincaid's lodgings, where it is difficult to dispel the odour of the butcher shop on the first floor. When Mrs Kincaid first meets Blakely, she vows to resist the temptation to exploit him; significantly, when she later yields to that temptation, the decision coincides with the shooting of a taxi driver, "the first murder since the cease-fires" (189). The first glimpse of Blakely's farm reveals two of his workers plucking slaughtered turkeys. The difficulties of mutual trust are symbolised in Blakely's immoderate discomfort when Mrs Kincaid gives him a bottle of whiskey: "He didn't want to accept a present from her. There was no call for her to give him a present. There was no call for her to come into the yard, looking for him" (78).

Significantly, when Mrs Kincaid broods upon her lost inheritance, she recalls the price the property fetched in 1968, one of the most politically resonant dates in Northern Ireland. This watershed year, in which the Civil Rights movement was suppressed and sectarian violence escalated, paving the way for British military occupation of the North, is also a watershed for Mrs Kincaid herself, and Trevor's interweaving of public and private history underscores the allegorical nature of the story. For both Mrs Kincaid and Northern Ireland, 1968 is a harbinger of catastrophe. But once again, Trevor avoids easy equations or predictable categories: Mrs Kincaid, an ageing woman bereft of her land, is no Poor Old Woman of popular Irish iconography. She is a Protestant whose exploitation had nothing to do with politics. By linking her situation with the problems of Northern Irish Catholics, Trevor at the same time challenges traditional boundaries and offers hope for the future.

Other signs of hope linger as well: the story takes place in early spring, and Blakely notes the ploughing of neighbouring fields. One of his customers joyfully announces his daughter's engagement. Mrs Kincaid wonders at Blakely's ability to go on with his life after the cruel murder of his family, and she thinks of how her own life might have been without the theft of her inheritance. When Blakely reluctantly accepts her gift of whiskey, the communal moment of their sharing a drink triggers childhood memories of his beloved brother, Willie John, who felt compelled to emigrate to America to escape the Troubles. The memory, significantly, is of how they flew their model airplanes, which despite getting tangled in nettles and running out of fuel, still survived, and the joy of the moment is imprinted deeply on Blakely's memory.

Likewise, new hope emerges out of disaster in the story's final scene. The catalyst for Mrs Kincaid's change of heart is an eruption of violence that threatens the survival of the peace process. "There had been murder and punishment, the burning of churches, violence again across the barricades of Drumcree, the destruction of the town of Omagh" (206). Trevor again makes reference to contemporary history here. In Drumcree, violence has on several occasions broken out as Catholics and Protestants have battled over pro-Unionist attempts to conduct Orange parades in Catholic neighbourhoods. Omagh was the site of a horrifying terrorist attack in August 1998, when an apparently misplaced car bomb killed 29 people, including nine children, a pregnant woman and her unborn twins. Hundreds of people were injured; several of the dead were from the same families. The violence of the attack riveted world attention, and its horror seemed at least temporarily to strengthen Northern Irish resolve to achieve a lasting peace.

Similarly, in Trevor's story, the terrible backslide into violence almost miraculously does not result in despair:

> Yet belief in the fragile peace persisted, too precious after so long to abandon. Stubbornly the people of the Troubles honoured the hope that had spread

among them, fierce in their clamour that it should
not go away. (206)

Trevor, who so often has depicted people seemingly unable
to escape history, apparently doomed to repeat its mistakes,
here offers hope for the future: "In spite of the quiet made
noisy again, its benign infection had reached out for Blakely;
it did so for Mrs Kincaid also, even though her trouble was
her own" (81). Mrs Kincaid, "weary at last of making entries
in a notebook", reaches out to the man she has wronged.

When Trevor received the David Cohen British Literature Prize in 1999, he requested that £10,000 of that award
be given to a young person from Omagh, to enable him or
her to pursue a career in writing fiction. This compassionate
gesture of faith to a community savaged by a brutal act of
political violence suggests Trevor's own willingness to bet
against the odds and in so doing turn a corner in his own
reading of Ireland's history.

The Hill Bachelors is more quietly rendered, more subtly
written, than much of Trevor's earlier fiction dealing with
Irish history and Irish politics. Gone are the dramatic moments of confrontation, the sometimes strident exposures
of painful truths, that characterised the earlier "Troubles"
stories. Characters are not compelled to repeat the errors
of the past, and though their predicaments may be difficult,
choice is possible. Guarded optimism has replaced the fatal-
ism of the past, and if characters are doomed to thwarted
lives, it is because they *choose* this fate.

Chapter Nine

Rewriting Trevor, Re-Imagining Ireland: *The Story of Lucy Gault*

In *The Story of Lucy Gault,* his first "Irish" novel since the 1994 *Felicia's Journey*, Trevor revisits earlier preoccupations. As in *Mrs Eckdorf in O'Neill's Hotel*, characters long for love and understanding; as in *Fools of Fortune*, chance plays cruel tricks; as in *The Silence in the Garden*, futile guilt results in near-self-immolation. Yet, as in *Felicia's Journey* and Trevor's recent stories, the past no longer has an inexorable stranglehold; old conceptions of Irish identity are shattered and reconstructed. In fact, *The Story of Lucy Gault* is filled with allusions to and even quotations from Trevor's earlier Irish fiction, playing new variations on his familiar themes. Like *Felicia's Journey*, *Lucy Gault* is undeniably allegorical. But Trevor is less concerned here with colonialism *per se* than with the issues of "making history" and defining Irish identity. By tweaking the predictable and diverting history from its usual course, this brilliant novel is less concerned with the repetitions of the past than it is with the fluidities of the future.

Trevor returns to the Big House milieu of *Fools of Fortune* and *The Silence in the Garden*, again covering an expanse of time from the early twentieth century to the present, including the Anglo-Irish War, the Irish Civil War, the emergence of the Free State and the Irish Republic. In this later novel, there is also glancing reference to the technological revolution wrought by computers, and the fading hegemony of the Catholic Church. Further, Trevor again sets the story in County Cork, revisiting a location that was both crucial in the Irish Civil War and in Trevor's personal history. In fact, *Lucy Gault* takes place in many of the scenes of Trevor's itinerant childhood: Lucy and her father visit the Mitchelstown Caves in the townland where Trevor was born; Lucy's lover, Ralph, is from Enniscorthy, where Trevor once lived; the natural beauty of coastal and provincial Cork, where Trevor spent part of his youth, is described in lyrical detail.

Further, this Big House, as in the two previous novels, has an English mistress. Heloise Gault blames her national origin for the attempted arson of Lahardane, her husband's family estate, believing that the presence of an English woman in the local Big House exacerbates already bitter feelings.

As in *Fools of Fortune*, chance is cruel in *Lucy Gault* — in a sense more bitterly cruel than in the previous novel. On the night of the attempted arson, Capt Everard Gault mistakenly shoots one of the would-be arsonists, wounding him slightly. In the nervy political climate of the early 1920s, Heloise fears for her family's safety and the Gaults decide to leave their beloved home, to the great distress of their eight-year-old daughter, Lucy, who runs away. Through a series of mischances, Lucy is feared drowned — her mother believes her to be a suicide — and the heartsick couple leaves Ireland for a peripatetic existence on the Continent, eventually settling in a small town in Italy until their anxiety about Mussolini's regime drives them to Switzerland. When Lucy is later discovered, nearly dead from hunger and exposure, the family servants, Henry and Bridget, and the Gaults' solicitor, Aloysius Sullivan, try in vain to locate them. For her part, Lucy grows up as a Wordsworthian Lucy, in a sense — isolated, lovely, and intimately connected to the natural world. But Lucy Gault is also a pariah: for many years local people condemn her thought-lessness in bringing such grief to her parents.

Lucy turns her guilt inward, and destructively so. Bewildered by her parents' failure to return, Lucy becomes, like the Rolleston children in *The Silence in the Garden*, self-flagellating, rejecting marriage to Ralph, the man she loves, because she feels responsible for her parents' exile, determined to await their return. In doing so, she lives a half-life, suspended in a nineteenth-century existence: with her affection for nature, her bee-keeping, she might be a Romantic heroine; her avid reading of Victorian novels and her painstaking needlework place her later in the century. Eccentrically dressed always in her mother's white clothes and with a life story that has evolved into a local legend, Lucy takes on the aura of a fairy-tale maiden, cast under a spell partially of her own making. The eruption of the Second World War has but a narrowly personal impact upon her: Ralph's enlistment in the army and her fear for his safety cause her to rethink her self-denying existence; yet chance is once again cruel, for Ralph, after many years of faithful love, has married someone else. When Everard returns to Lahardane after his wife's death, he and Lucy must settle for "what there was" (*LG*, 194): after so many years, they cannot recapture the easy intimacy of Lucy's childhood, and just when they begin to break through the awkwardness between them, Everard dies.

The bare bones of the novel's plot seem crushingly sad, yet *The Story of Lucy Gault* is ultimately not a tragedy, nor is the novel only one woman's story; it is Ireland's. In personal terms, something is salvaged from so much unnecessary suffering. Chance is not unrelentingly cruel: Henry discovers the lost Lucy by accident, drawn to a usually unfrequented spot while he is searching for stones to repair a wall; Ralph stumbles upon Lahardane while exploring the countryside, and even though their relationship is eventually broken, Lucy would be the poorer for not having experienced Ralph's love. Despite their inability to recover emotionally from the loss of their only child, a loss compounded by Heloise's several miscarriages and eventual inability to have more children, the Gaults share an extraordinarily loving marriage. Though their first names punningly recall the tragic lovers Heloise and Abelard, the Gaults share an intimacy that sustains them through Heloise's persistent depression and self-blame for what she believes to be Lucy's self-destruction. Indeed, Trevor, who more often has written about unhappy marriages, perhaps inspired by his own parents' union, of which he has stated, "'Strindberg would have been very excited by their marriage'" (Ní Anluain, 234), here seems closer to his own happy 50-year marriage to Jane Ryan.

In fact, *Lucy Gault* is perhaps the most autobiographical of Trevor's fictions. Ralph once attended boarding school in the Dublin mountains, as did Trevor; like Trevor's own father, Ralph's employer works for a bank. The happiest times in the Gaults' lives after Lucy's disappearance take place in Italy, a country for which Trevor has a deep affection and in which he has set much of his fiction.

English by birth, Irish by marriage, Heloise feels most at home in Italy, drawn to its art, particularly paintings of the Annunciation, fascinated by the lives of the saints who inspired the painters. Annunciations figure largely in Trevor's previous writing, particularly in the collection *After Rain*, though Trevor's annunciations, like Joyce's epiphanies, are often triggered by mundane events. Heloise, both in her comment to her husband that "'Love is greedy when it is starved. . . . Love is beyond all reason when it is starved'" (172), and her fascination with saints, unwittingly forges a connection to the daughter who will remain in her mind forever a child.

Lucy's own love for Ralph verges on "greedy" and "beyond all reason" after her father's return. She writes to Ralph, still loving him, and hoping that he will leave his marriage for her. Yet despite his desire to return to Lucy and to

Lahardane, Ralph is a man of honour and remains in Enniscorthy with his wife and child, running the family sawmill and seeking solace in nature.

If Lucy embodies the pitfalls of love that her mother had described, she also plays a variation on her mother's fascination with saints, a fascination more earthly than spiritual. As Everard recalls to Aloysius Sullivan, "She [Heloise] wondered about the nature of St Thomas's doubt. Or if Tobias' angel had taken the form of a bird. Or how on earth St Simeon managed on his pillar'" (159). Just as her mother was drawn to the quotidian existence of the saints, Lucy in her middle years becomes a kind of secular saint.

When Everard returns to Lahardane, so does Horahan, the young man he once shot. Filled with stories about the evils of the Big House, ironically, by the clergymen who taught him, Horahan stumbled into the arson scheme, and his life has been blighted by the experience. His lack of political commitment is evident; what is apparent is that the experience at Lahardane has unhinged his sanity. Just as Heloise mistakenly believes Lucy to be a suicide, Horahan believes the arson scheme succeeded; like Imelda in *Fools of Fortune*, he is haunted by visions of a burning house and a dead child, visions so graphic and tortuous that he eventually becomes a patient at the local asylum. Another of Trevor's many characters who feel compelled to reveal uncomfortable truths, Horahan before his complete breakdown secretly watches Lucy, then arrives at Lahardane to unburden himself to her father, to seek understanding. Despite the catastrophic results of Horahan's past actions, Everard treats him compassionately; Lucy is devastated: "For a moment she looked into the features of the man who had returned after so long and saw there only madness. No meaning dignified his return; no order patterned, as perhaps it might have, past and present; no sense was made of anything" (191). In a terrible moment of despair — a bitter annunciation — she sees the futility of her life exposed.

Yet, as in the end of *Fools of Fortune*, something is salvaged, for after her father's death Lucy does not immerse herself in bitterness. She returns to the scenes of her parents' travels; she visits her mother's grave; she renounces her love for Ralph. She is also drawn to Horahan. First she sends him one of her exquisite needlework pieces; symbolically, it is a field of poppies, the flowers of remembrance, recalling also her father, a veteran of the First World War. Lucy eventually becomes Horahan's regular visitor at the asylum, and though he does not recognise her, her visits and their regular matches of the childhood board game Snakes and Ladders comfort him. Their choice of pastime is significant, for Snakes and Ladders was originally a game of morality; as the *Oxford English Dictionary* notes, "snakes and ladders" evolved into an adjective to describe life's vicissitudes — highly appropriate in this novel of chance and mischance.

But unlike the elderly Quintons and their mad child Imelda at the end of *Fools of Fortune*, Lucy's fate is less pathetic. In 1950s Ireland, Lucy of the Big House is now closely aligned with the middle class Protestant "remnant" that Trevor has so often written about in his accounts of the early years of the Republic of Ireland. That Lucy faithfully visits the Catholic Horahan, that she eventually walks behind his coffin in public mourning, has far-reaching effects upon the community. As Trevor has so often noted, the "small gesture" is important. In Lucy's old age, she is befriended by two nuns who visit her regularly, tend to her needs, and grow to love the serene beauty of Lahardane. To the nuns, Lucy is an extraordinary mystery: out of her "calamity" has come redemption in the form of her kindness to its catalyst, Horahan. Yet though Sisters Antony and Mary Bartholomew find common ground with Lucy in their mutual liking, in their shared stories, Lucy sees her life as no mystery but rather a series of "chances". Like the Protestant governess Anna Maria Heddoe's sharing the story of the True Cross with Fogarty, who passes the tale on to the Catholic servants in the Pulvertaft household, Lucy, too, bridges the two religions by acquainting the nuns with the story of Saint Cecilia, the patron of Montemarmoreo, the Italian town so beloved by her parents.

Though Trevor has used saints' names and saintly figures in his Irish fiction before — one thinks of Attracta, for instance, a modern-day Protestant schoolteacher who tries to turn her pupils away from violence — Lucy, though both her name and her actions are saintly, is no saint. Though Lucy's name means "light", St Lucy is the patron saint of the blind, long prayed-to for vision problems. Lucy Gault for much of her life suffers from a kind of blurred vision, as evidenced in her misguided self-sacrifice. And though the community marvels at her ability to reach out to Horahan, Trevor does not indicate that she does so out of holiness. As we have seen, when Horahan first returns to Lahardane, Lucy has a traumatic existential moment, the revelation that her life has been meaningless. In the wake of her parents' death and her awareness that Ralph is unattainable, Lucy needs to impose some kind of order or purpose onto her lonely existence. And throughout, she keeps her own counsel, remaining enigmatic not only to the local community but to the reader as well. Well aware that her behaviour has been a source of wonder, she thinks, ". . . does it matter, really, why people visit one another or walk behind a coffin, only that they do?" (223).

Trevor's tendency to avoid easy categorisations in his depictions of Irish people is especially evident in *The Story of Lucy Gault*. At the time of the attempted arson, Everard Gault is a modest man who works alongside his servant, repairing the roof lead, replacing the window glass, keeping the deteriorating house going. Unlike the English Mr Pulvertaft from *The News from Ireland*, who justifies his recent windfall in the shape of an inherited Irish estate with a kind of "white man's burden" explanation that he feels obligated to "save" the place, Everard's family has lived in Lahardane since the

early eighteenth century; much of the family history is un-
known, but at various times both the Lord Lieutenant and
Daniel O'Connell have been guests at the house. Horahan is
not a nationalist fighting for his principles but rather a con-
fused, easily led boy.

The historical span of the novel is vast: between them,
Lucy and her father experience two world wars and two
Irish wars; the decline of the Big House; the founding of
modern Ireland. Trevor foregrounds personal history, however, realistically showing that for most of us world events
are shaped in our consciousness by our personal experiences: for Everard and Heloise Gault, the rise of Mussolini
means the necessary departure from their beloved Italy; after
Heloise's death, when Everard passes through London, he
thinks of the "drab post-war capital" that "victory seemed
more like bad-tempered submission. . . ." Playing on Blake's
"London", Trevor suggests that "Dreariness was everywhere, in every face, in every gesture"; the only exceptions
are the "jolly" "street-corner spivs" and "sweetly scented
tarts" (148) — and considering that a "spiv" is a dodgy character and the "tarts" are probably not a reference to pastry,
it's rather cold comfort. Similarly, when Lahardane's history
is recalled, alongside such big events as Daniel O'Connell's
visit, "as well-remembered, as often talked about, were births
and marriages and deaths, domestic incidents, changes and
additions to this room or that, occasions of anger or reconciliation" (5). The year 1847 was the worst of the Potato
Famine; it is also recalled in the Gault family history as the
year an ancestor suffered a stroke.

Trevor does not suggest here, as he has in earlier works
such as *The News from Ireland*, that such focus on personal
history in the midst of world-altering events is self-indulgent.
Rather, he posits the tenacity of life in the midst of cata-
clysm. In some of his earlier Irish works, characters were
trapped in history, seemingly doomed to repeat it or to

witness its repetitions, as does the eponymous Attracta or Willie Quinton in *Fools of Fortune*. In *The Story of Lucy Gault*, Trevor breaks down predictable patterns, grounds his characters historically without enslaving them to history.

For instance, despite the terrible consequences, the attempted burning of Lahardane does not end as it might — and as it does in Horahan's anguished imaginings. In *Fools of Fortune*, the house burns, family members and servants die; a son's life is blighted by bloodthirsty revenge; his daughter is driven mad, in part by her mother's violent imagination. In *The Story of Lucy Gault*, despite their sad disappointments, Everard and Heloise die peacefully; Lucy turns away from her bitterness and finds serenity. Violence is not inevitable.

Along the way, Trevor scrambles and deconstructs Irish history, breaking the pattern. When Henry discovers the barely alive Lucy, she is described thus: "The child's lips were stained with blackberry juice. There was a sick look about her, her cheeks fallen in, dark hollows beneath her eyes, her hair as ragged as a tinker's" (40). The passage is a chilling echo of Famine-era accounts of starving children, but here the Big House child becomes a reincarnation of the Famine child. Further, when Lucy returns home, Bridget and Henry move into the Big House to care for her, and remain there permanently. As they become more infirm with age, Lucy, now the mistress of the Big House, becomes their caretaker and, out of consideration for them, eats her meals with them in the kitchen. Lucy's lover, Ralph, an ineffectual tutor waiting to take over the family sawmill, also recalls Irish history. From Enniscorthy, Ralph talks of his hometown as well as Gorey and Ferns, all three key sites in the 1798 rebellion. But Ralph's Enniscorthy has little connection with the violent past, the terrible slaughter at Vinegar Hill: he manages a sawmill and indulges his love of nature by reforesting barren ground.

Just as Trevor rewrites and revises his own *oeuvre* in this novel, playing variations on his earlier Irish works, even quoting them (as when Everard wonders about "'the news from Ireland'"), he plays new variations on Yeats. In *Fools of Fortune*, the mentally disturbed yet saintly Imelda uses Yeats's "The Lake Isle of Innisfree" as a mantra of sorts, yet the poem's ability to give her solace evaporates in the face of her growing awareness of violence and horror. "Innisfree" returns in *The Story of Lucy Gault* in the sense that Lucy lives the poem: she keeps a "hive for the honey-bee"; and though Lahardane is built on a much grander scale than Yeats's longed-for clay-and-wattle confection, Lucy's life there is notable for its tranquillity and isolation.

Yet just as Yeats in later life spurned this early, romantic poem, Trevor through Lucy argues the limits of the poem's modest utopia: the hives are eventually derelict; Lucy breaks her isolation. Trevor substitutes another Yeatsian trope in tracing Lucy's later life, in which "The Wild Swans at Coole" reverberates. When Ralph first courts Lucy, he wonders at her unfamiliarity with the local town, Enniseala ("swan island"). Only after her father's return does Lucy become a regular visitor to the town; the swans who have given their name to the place continue to delight her even in old age, when she can no longer visit them. The nuns' response to her inquiries about the birds, that "'They're still there always'" (223), echoes Yeats's symbolic linking of the Coole swans with immortality, a beautiful constant amidst the flux of human life. But Yeats's swans inhabited Coole Park, the Gregory estate that for him embodied the ceremonious grace of Ascendancy life. Significantly, when Lucy Gault encounters her swans, it is because she has left the Big House and begun to enter the world of middle-class, Catholic Ireland. As an old woman, Lucy hopes the swans will always inhabit Enniseala; in speaking with the nuns, she privately thinks that just as her Ascendancy world has eroded, so too will the Catholic Ireland in which their lives are grounded, part of the inevitable shifts and fluctuations of history.

Finally, just as Trevor has throughout his Irish fiction subverted the popular use of female icons to symbolise Ireland itself, exposing the ugly underside of reducing women to romantic Cathleens and pathetic old women, in his final image of Lucy he leaves us with a new variation on an old symbol. The novel ends quietly, with the now-elderly Lucy sitting alone, having walked the grounds of her beloved estate and contemplated the decaying house. She knows that Lahardane's days, like hers, are numbered, and the house will probably become a private hotel. Though she privately believes she should have died as a child, she takes solace in gazing at the blue hydrangeas that once delighted her mother. With a life spanning the emergence of modern Ireland and waning in the shadow of the Celtic Tiger, Lucy is a very different "poor old woman", a caveat against reliving the past, clinging to futile myths and outmoded images.

That Trevor revisits so much familiar ground in *Lucy Gault* is in no way indicative of failing creative powers. The novel reveals its author both "rewriting" Ireland and rewriting himself. Plot elements from earlier works are revisited yet given a different outcome; language is echoed with telling reverberations: when Everard wonders about the "news from Ireland" he is thinking about the life he sadly abandoned for years of unwilling exile. But Trevor's choice to echo his earlier work about the Famine is entirely appropriate, for though the "news" Everard anticipates is undramatic — how Henry and Bridget are faring, how the farm is getting along, etc. — the actual news he receives only much later is personally earth-shattering, the choice of language symbolically apt. In this allegorical rendering of Ireland's history, the "news" of the Famine and the "news" of Lucy's survival and the "news" of Irish independence are inextricably connected. Further, Heloise's grief over Lucy's assumed death causes her to turn her back on Ireland: she no longer cares about the "news" from a place she has come to loathe. Yet Trevor makes it clear that this English mistress of an Irish estate, by blaming Ireland for her misery, contributes to that misery's continuance: Everard writes numerous letters to Ireland but will not post them because he thinks it would be an act of betrayal to his wife, thus unwittingly prolonging the discovery that Lucy is still alive.

. And though *Lucy Gault* is filled with the same kind of drama, personal suffering, and world-wrenching events that inform earlier works, Trevor's increasingly understated style, eschewing the dramatic outbursts of Cynthia in "Beyond the Pale", Attracta, Fogarty and other characters compelled to shock their listeners into realisation, carries its own emotional punch: as in "Events at Drimaghleen" and *Felicia's Journey*, extraordinary, sometimes appalling events occur in the calmest, most uninflected language. As Thomas Mallon noted in his review of the novel:

> There is no quieter narrative voice than Trevor's impersonal but irreducible one, and none that so demands a reader's strict attention. Enormities come without warning, never a decibel louder than anything else. . . . (9)

For instance, Everard's death is revealed thus: "Later he was aware of pain. It did not wake him" (198); Heloise's heartbreaking miscarriage and her discovery that she can have no more children is folded into a paragraph describing a clockwork toy given to her by her husband.

Further, Trevor's prose, usually notable for its clarity and precision, becomes more elliptical, more complex. In this novel that avoids easy answers, Trevor compels the reader to wrestle with his prose and sometimes to remain stranded in ambiguity. When Horahan visits Everard, he reveals that after Lucy's disappearance his status in the community took a downturn: once praised for his heroism in attempting to burn Lahardane, he has now become a figure of shame:

> "There's no one would say it, sir. The girl you were going with wouldn't say it on account it was too terrible to say to any man. The same as there's people in Enniseala wouldn't say it yet. In a shop they wouldn't. Not my mother herself in her lifetime, God rest her. Nor the lads above at the Camp." (186)

Everard is unsuccessful in finding out what Horahan is talking about — and so are we. Perhaps he refers to his belief that he has indeed committed both arson and murder; but Trevor never specifies.

Less stylistically difficult but similarly inconclusive is Trevor's description of the impact of Everard's return upon Lahardane.

> . . . the events since the night he had aimed his rifle from an upstairs window had not become a chronicle as they had elsewhere. They had not even been tidily put together for the sake of their retelling, but in memory remained haphazard, as they had happened. Nor was the upheaval occasioned by the Captain's return, and the news he brought of his widowing, taken to be the completion of a pattern of events, as they were assumed to be elsewhere. (155)

Life resists logical patterning; history is not a logical progression but a palimpsest, symbolised by the fact that visitors to Enniseala can still see the pre-Independence royal insignia lurking behind the green paint of the Republic's postal boxes. And though Everard had once told the child Lucy that "'The past was the enemy in Ireland'" (10), after Lucy's disappearance the omniscient narrator makes it quite clear that blaming history will not do:

... he tried not to wonder if there was punishment in this. For had not, after all, the people risen up, and was not that the beginning of the hell which had so swiftly been completed in this small corner? He could not know that, as certainly as the truth had no place in an erroneous assumption, so it had none in such fearful conjectures of damnation. Chance, not wrath, had this summer ordered the fate of the Gaults. (36)

As he had in such earlier works as "Teresa's Wedding" and *Felicia's Journey*, Trevor also juxtaposes discordant elements for ironic effect: just as the surface jollity of Teresa's wedding is undercut by deflationary language, and Hilditch's plans to abduct and possibly murder Felicia are given a romantic soundtrack, Lucy's and Ralph's romantic illusions are linguistically punctured by mundane details. The married Ralph daydreams about Lucy while a landscaper outlines his plan to more easily exterminate troublesome rabbits by first blinding them with bright headlights. As Lucy sits with her father in a hotel lounge and indulges in wild dreams that Ralph can abandon his life in Enniscorthy and join her at Lahardane, the scene is counterpointed by an elderly man's fussing that his hens have disgraced him by bringing fleas into the house.

Though much of Trevor's earlier Irish fiction was marked by moments of truth, characters such as Fogarty "rapping out" unpleasant realities needing to be acknowledged, the Gaults are closer to the Pulvertafts in their affinity for silence. As Robert Rhodes has pointed out, the Pulvertaft household is marked by an avoidance of unpleasant realities; the Gaults, too, often leave their deepest feelings unsaid. Everard is aware of his daughter's grief over Ralph, but he never broaches the subject. He silently berates himself for withholding from the child Lucy the truth about their departure from Lahardane, feeling he might have prevented her running away. Lucy resists the impulse to tell Horahan of the disaster his actions have generated. Horahan himself lapses into silence after unburdening himself to Everard, and he remains silent for the rest of his life.

The absence in Trevor's recent Irish fiction of the intentionally strident verbal eruptions and shocking acts of violence that characterised, in varying ways, *Mrs Eckdorf*, *Fools of Fortune*, *The Silence in the Garden* and several of the author's "Troubles" stories, signals a subtle sea change in the author's perception of Ireland. Critics have noted that the contemporary Ireland of Celtic Tiger, mobile phone and software receives only the most glancing attention from Trevor, as when an otherwise admiring Atom Egoyan asserted that the setting in *Felicia's Journey*, despite its contemporary time, was an Ireland that no longer exists. Trevor's long expatriation, despite his frequent visits to Ireland, has been duly noted, sometimes with the suggestion that the author is out of tune with contemporary Ireland. Trevor frequently sets his Irish works in the past, whether the past he personally remembers from his youth or the historical past that continues to compel him emotionally and intellectually.

It would be wrong to conclude, however, that Trevor is out of tune with contemporary Ireland, for his Irish fiction touches the pulse of current preoccupations with identity, how to interpret history, how to square Ireland's past with Ireland's future. Trevor's is a complex vision, his Irish fiction a sustained lesson on the dual dangers of repeating or forgetting the past, the inevitability of mythmaking and the necessity to remain uncontrolled by traditional images, an acknowledgement of the ease with which groups of people may be categorised and the urgency of resisting such stereotyping.

Contemporary critics such as Declan Kiberd, Shaun Richards and David Cairns have argued that Ireland should extricate itself from past confining, unimaginative definitions of identity. "In one sense then a *tabula rasa* cleared of disabling shibboleths is being advocated as the prerequisite for the foundation of a secure Irish cultural identity which transcends disabling divisions" (Cairns and Richards: 1988, 49). Kiberd advocates an abandonment of the "binary thinking" that forces people into predetermined categories and thus discourages change. Cairns and Richards conclude:

> The relationship of England and Ireland, coloniser and colonised, Unionist and Nationalist, within a small western European archipelago has to be re-thought and re-read, and art and culture on all dimensions and levels of complexity must seek to provide the single word-spark to an inextinguishable thought. (1988: 154)

Yet what literary critics have failed to acknowledge is that William Trevor recognised the complexities of Irish identity long before many contemporary theorists began to dissect them. Further, Irishness is for Trevor a much more inclusive term than is often allowed by these pathologists, for women have always had a voice in Trevor's Irish fiction, their silencing and stereotyping consistently deplored. Nor has the author's embracing of a diverse Ireland concealed an agenda to revise the past out of all recognition or to privilege the narratives of any one group.

Indeed, *The Story of Lucy Gault* calls into question the very business of what Brian Friel has called "making history". All the denizens of Lahardane recognise that their lives have been buffeted about by chance, that logic and pattern has no place in their misery or their happiness. But the community at large feels compelled to historicise Lahardane, to impose upon the Gaults' lives a symbolic meaning, a myth. When the Gaults first depart Ireland, they are viewed as justifiably punished for the Ascendancy usurpation they symbolise. With the compassion engendered by independence and passing time, Lucy is variously seen as a pitiable figure, an oddity — "the Protestant woman" in a Catholic-dominated land — and a saintly peacemaker. Horahan is at first praised for his part in driving the Gaults from Lahardane, but as news of their tragedy unfolds he becomes a pariah. Trevor emphasises that historical memory is fickle and deceptive:

> Borrowed facts, sewn in where there was a dearth, gathered authority with repetition. Stirred by what was told of the events at Lahardane, memories strayed into other houses, through other family archives. . . . In talk inspired by what was told, the subtleties that clogged the tidiness of narration were smudged away. The spare reality of what had happened was coloured and enriched, and altogether made better. (70)

In other words, the invented history, the narrative constructed out of random events, is ultimately more satisfying than the chaotic reality on which it is based. Humanity desires logical explanations, hankers after pattern and design. But just as Lucy herself realises that over time she will evolve from local legend into enduring myth, and that every public version of her life is suspect, we as readers are prodded into questioning this very process by which events are transformed into "history".

The Story of Lucy Gault is Trevor's subtlest, most complex reading of Ireland. It asks the questions: if written history and the myths is supports are suspect, then what is Ireland and who are the Irish? Lucy's ultimate acceptance of change, her ability to extricate herself from the past without forgetting it, moves her beyond the "remnant" status she has come to occupy in an evolving nation. This "old woman" is no idealised icon, but rather the hopeful face of Ireland's future.

Bibliography

Selected Works by William Trevor

Trevor, William (1996), *After Rain*, London: Viking.

Trevor, William (1975), *Angels at the Ritz and Other Stories*, London: Bodley Head.

Trevor, William (1972), *The Ballroom of Romance and Other Stories*, London: Bodley Head.

Trevor, William (1981), *Beyond the Pale*, London: Bodley Head.

Trevor, William (1997), "Big Bucks", *The New Yorker*, Vol. LXII, 10 Feb., pp. 68–73.

Trevor, William (1965), *The Boarding House*, London: Bodley Head.

Trevor, William (1976), *The Children of Dynmouth*, London: Bodley Head.

Trevor, William (1992), *The Collected Stories*, London: Viking

Trevor, William (1967), *The Day We Got Drunk on Cake and Other Stories*, London: Bodley Head.

Trevor, William (1998), *Death in Summer*, London: Viking.

Trevor, William (1979), *The Distant Past*, Dublin: Poolbeg Press.

Trevor, William (1973), *Elizabeth Alone*, London: Bodley Head.

Trevor, William (1993), *Excursions in the Real World: Memoirs*, London: Hutchinson; (1994), New York: Alfred A. Knopf.

Trevor, William (1990), *Family Sins*, London: Bodley Head; (1990), New York: Viking.

Trevor, William (1994), *Felicia's Journey*, London: Viking.

Trevor, William (1983), *Fools of Fortune*, London: Bodley Head; New York: Viking.

Trevor, William (2000), *The Hill Bachelors*, London: Viking.

Trevor, William (1995), *Ireland: Selected Stories*, London: Penguin.

Trevor, William (1992), *Juliet's Story*, London: Bodley Head.

Trevor, William (1966), *The Love Department*, London: Bodley Head.

Trevor, William (1978), *Lovers of Their Time*, London: Bodley Head.

Trevor, William (1971), *Miss Gomez and the Brethren*, London: Bodley Head.

Trevor, William (1969), *Mrs Eckdorf in O'Neill's Hotel*, London: Bodley Head; New York: Viking.

Trevor, William (1986), *The News from Ireland and Other Stories*, London: Bodley Head, 1986; New York, Viking.

Trevor, William (1987), *Nights at the Alexandra*, London: Hutchinson.

Trevor, William (1964), *The Old Boys*, London: Bodley Head.

Trevor, William (1992), *Outside Ireland: Selected Stories*, London: Penguin.

Trevor, William, Ed. (1989), *The Oxford Book of Irish Short Stories*, Oxford University Press.

Trevor, William (1981), "Saints", *Atlantic Monthly* Vol. 247, January, pp. 29-36.

Trevor, William (1981), *Scenes from an Album*, Dublin: Co-op Books.

Trevor, William (1988), *The Silence in the Garden*, London: Bodley Head; New York: Penguin.

Trevor, William (1958), *A Standard of Behaviour*, London: Hutchinson.

Trevor, William (1983), *The Stories of William Trevor*, London: Penguin.

Trevor, William (2002), *The Story of Lucy Gault*, London: Viking, 2002.

Trevor, William (1991), *Two Lives: Reading Turgenev and My House in Umbria*, London: Viking.

Trevor, William (1984), *A Writer's Ireland: Landscape in Literature*, London: Thames & Hudson; New York: Viking.

Interviews with William Trevor

Aronson, Jacqueline Stahl (1987), "William Trevor: An Interview", *Irish Literary Supplement* Vol. 7, No. 2, Spring, pp. 7–8.

Ní Anluain, Clíodhna (2000) (editor), *Reading the Future: Irish Writers in Conversation with Mike Murphy*, Dublin: Lilliput, pp. 222–239.

Stout, Mira (1989–90), "The Art of Fiction CVIII: William Trevor", *Paris Review* Vol. 110, spring, pp. 119–151.

Books on William Trevor

MacKenna, Dolores (1999), *William Trevor: The Writer and His Work*, Dublin: New Island Books.

Morrison, Kristin (1993), *William Trevor*, New York: Twayne.

Paulson, Suzanne Morrow (1993), *William Trevor: A Study of the Short Fiction*, New York: Twayne.

Schirmer, Gregory A. (1990), *William Trevor: A Study of His Fiction*, London: Routledge.

Critical Books, Articles, Chapters, etc.

Allen, Bruce (1993), "William Trevor and Other People's Worlds", *Sewanee Review*, Vol. CI, No. 1, pp. 138–44.

Baldwin, James (1965), "Sonny's Blues", *Going to Meet the Man*, New York: Dial Press, pp. 101–41.

Boland, Eavan (1995), "Outside History", *Object Lessons: The Life of the Woman and the Poet in Our Time*, New York: Norton, pp. 123–53.

Bowman, James, (1995), Review of *Felicia's Journey*, by William Trevor, *National Review*, 6 March, p. 67.

Bruckner, D.J.R. (1990), "Stories Keep Coming to a Late-Blooming Writer", *New York Times*, 21 May, C11, p. 14.

Butler, Alban (1985), "St Rose of Viterbo, Virgin", *Lives of the Saints*, Concise Edition, Michael Walsh (editor), New York: Harper & Row, pp. 275–6.

Cahalan, James (1999), *Double Visions: Women and Men in Modern and Contemporary Irish Fiction*, Syracuse: Syracuse UP.

Cairns, David and Shaun Richards (1988), *Writing Ireland: Colonialism, Nationalism, and Culture*, Manchester: Manchester UP.

Caldwell, Gail, (1995), "William Trevor's Lonely Sojourn", Review of *Felicia's Journey*, by William Trevor, *The Boston Sunday Globe*, 8 January, pp. 47, 49.

Christensen, Lis and Lis Pihl (1989), "History and Self-Deception in Two of William Trevor's Irish Stories", *Literatur in Wissenschaft und Unterricht*, Vol. 22, No. 3, pp. 207-17.

Core, George (1993), "'Belonging Nowhere, Seeing Everywhere': William Trevor and the Art of Distance", *Hollins Critic*, Vol. XXX, No. 4, pp. 2–11.

Craig, Patricia (1994), Review of *Felicia's Journey*, by William Trevor, *New Statesman and Society*, Vol. 19, August, p. 37.

Curtis, L. Perry, Jr. (1971), *Apes and Angels: The Irishman in Victorian Caricature*, Washington, DC: Smithsonian Institution Press.

Deane, Seamus (1977), "The Literary Myths of the Revival: A Case for Their Abandonment", *Myth and Reality in Irish Literature*, Joseph Ronsley (editor), Waterloo, Ontario, Canada: Wilfrid Laurier Press, pp. 317–29.

Donnelly, James S., Sr. (1989), "The Administration of relief, 1846–7", *A New History of Ireland*, W.E. Vaughan (editor), Vol. V: "Ireland Under the Union I: 1801–70", Oxford: Clarendon Press.

Foster, John Wilson (1990), *Colonial Consequences: Essays in Irish Literature and Culture*, Dublin: Lilliput, 1990.

Foster, John Wilson (1991), Introduction to William Trevor, "Beyond the Pale", *The Field Day Anthology of Irish Writing*, Vol. III, Seamus Deane (general editor), Derry: Field Day Publications, pp. 1385–6.

Friel, Brian (1984), *Selected Plays*, Seamus Deane (introduction), Washington, DC: The Catholic University of America Press.

Gitzen, Julian (1979), "The Truth-Tellers of William Trevor", *Critique*, Vol. 21, No. 1, pp. 59–72.

Gordon, Mary (1991), "William Trevor's *Fools of Fortune*", *Good Boys and Dead Girls and Other Essays*, New York: Viking, pp. 45–51.

Graeber, Laurel (1995), "'Almost Everything Happens By Chance'", *New York Times Book Review*, 8 January 1995, p. 22.

Harte, Liam and Lance Pettitt (2000), "States of Dislocation: William Trevor's *Felicia's Journey* and Maurice Leitch's *Gilchrist*", *Comparing Postcolonial Literatures: Dislocations*, Ashok Bery and Patricia Murray (editors), London: Macmillan, pp. 70–80.

Haughey, Jim (1995), "Joyce and Trevor's Dubliners: The Legacy of Colonialism", *Studies in Short Fiction*, Vol. 32, No. 3, pp. 355–365.

Innes, C.L. (1993), *Woman and Nation in Irish Literature and Society, 1880–1935*, Athens: Univ. of Georgia Press.

Keating, H.R.F. (1982), *Whodunit? A Guide to Crime, Suspense, & Spy Fiction*, New York: Van Nostrand Reinhold Co.

Kiberd, Declan (1995), *Inventing Ireland: The Literature of the Modern Nation*, Cambridge: Harvard Univ. Press.

Kreilkamp, Vera (1998), *The Anglo-Irish Novel and the Big House*, Syracuse: Syracuse Univ. Press.

Larsen, Max Deen (1992), "Saints of the Ascendancy: William Trevor's Big-House Novels", *Ancestral Voices: The Big House in Anglo-Irish Literature*, Otto Rauchbauer (editor), Hildesheim: Olm, pp. 257–77.

Longley, Edna (1994), *The Living Stream: Literature and Revisionism in Ireland*, Newcastle Upon Tyne: Bloodaxe Books.

Mallon, Thomas (2003) "Fools of Fortune", Review of *The Story of Lucy Gault*, by William Trevor, *New York Times Book Review*, 29 September, p. 9.

McGrath, Patrick (1995), "Never Did Spider More Hungrily Wait", Review of *Felicia's Journey*, by William Trevor, *New York Times Book Review*, 8 January 1995, pp. 1, 22.

Memmi, Albert (1965), *The Coloniser and the Colonised*, Jean-Paul Sartre (introduction), Howard Greenfield (translator), Boston: Beacon Press.

Morrison, Kristin (1991), "The Family Sins of Social and Political Evils", *Irish Literary Supplement*, Vol. 10, No. 1, Spring, p. 20.

Morrissey, Thomas (1990), "Trevor's *Fools of Fortune*: The Rape of Ireland", *Notes on Modern Irish Literature*, Vol. 2, pp. 58–60.

Mother Ireland (1988), Anne Crilly (director), Derry Film and Video.

Ní Dhomhnaill, Nuala (1996), "What Foremothers?" The Comic Tradition in Irish Women Writers, Theresa O'Connor (editor), Gainesville: University Press of Florida, pp. 8–20.

Ó Gráda, Cormac (1989), *The Great Irish Famine*, London: Macmillan.

Parkin, Andrew (1988), "Shadows of Destruction: The Big House in Contemporary Irish Fiction", *Cultural Contexts and Literary Idioms in Contemporary Irish Literature*, Michael Kenneally (editor), Totowa, New Jersey: Barnes and Noble, pp. 306–35.

Ponsford, Michael (1988), "Only the Truth: The Short Stories of William Trevor", *Éire-Ireland*, Vol. XXIII, No. 1, Spring, pp. 75–86.

Porton, Richard (1999), "The Politics of Denial: An Interview with Atom Egoyan", *Cineaste*, Vol. 25, No. 1, pp. 39–41.

Reynolds, Lorna (1983), "Irish Women in Legend, Literature and Life", *Woman in Irish Legend, Life and Literature*, S. F. Gallagher (editor), Totowa, New Jersey: Barnes and Noble, pp. 11–25.

Rhodes, Robert (1989), "'The Rest Is Silence': Secrets in Some William Trevor Stories", *New Irish Writing: Essays in Memory of Raymond J. Porter*, James D. Brophy and Eamon Grennan (editors), Boston: G.K. Hall, pp. 35–53.

Rhodes, Robert (1983), "William Trevor's Stories of the Troubles", *Contemporary Irish Writing*, James D. Brophy and Raymond J. Porter (editors), Boston: Iona College Press/Twayne, pp. 95–114.

Symons, Julian (1985), *Bloody Murder: From the Detective Story to the Crime Novel*, 2nd ed., New York: Viking.

Tracy, Robert (2002), "Telling Tales: The Fictions of William Trevor", *Colby Quarterly*, Vol. XXXVIII, No. 3, pp. 295–307.

Wilson, Rebecca E. (1990), "Eavan Boland", *Sleeping with Monsters: Conversations with Scottish and Irish Woman Poets*, Gillean Somerville-Arjat and Rebecca E. Wilson (editors), Dublin: Wolfhound Press, pp. 79–90.

Index